PKI Implementation and Infrastructures

The concept of a PKI (public key infrastructure) has been around for decades, but it is one strand of IT which has taken an extraordinarily long time to come to fruition within the mainstream. This is mostly because implementing a PKI is time consuming and difficult. Maintaining a PKI is equally time consuming and even more difficult within the real world of mergers and acquisitions against a backdrop of ever-changing technology. Many organisations simply give up and hand everything over to a third party who promises to manage everything on their behalf. This is generally not a good idea and simply delays the inevitability of failures and misunderstood complexity. This book explores all the aspects of implementing and maintaining a PKI that the other books on the subject seem to miss. It reflects decades of hard-won experience, not only in PKI, not only in IT, not only in electronics, but in business, government agencies and academia alike. The book also explores the existence of a PKI alongside other technologies, such as biometrics, and against an ever-changing world of development methodologies. This last point is particularly relevant at this time as we are in the middle of a quiet, but all encompassing revolution in this respect. Consequently, this is the *one* book on PKI that you have to have on your shelf, whether you be a company director, IT manager, government minister or teacher of IT. It is the book which fills in all the gaps left in the literature and treads paths which others fear to tread. You will enjoy it enormously if you are from an IT background.

Julian Ashbourn is a prolific literary author with many popular titles in both the arts and sciences, including poetry and philosophy. He is also an experienced audio engineer and a composer with more than 50 full-scale symphonic works to his credit, in addition to other genres. Julian is also a qualified geoscientist and loves nature and anything within the natural world or connected with the sciences. In the IT field, Julian is an acknowledged expert on biometrics, encryption and infrastructure. He has had a varied career, working all over the world, often troubleshooting systems, from Arabia and Africa to Australia, Russia, Japan and almost every European country. The last 20 years of his career were spent in the aviation industry where he supported projects around a very large IT infrastructure, working on just about every scenario including, of course, PKI.

PKI Implementation and Infrastructures

Julian Ashbourn

CRC Press
Taylor & Francis Group
Boca Raton London New York

CRC Press is an imprint of the
Taylor & Francis Group, an **informa** business

First edition published 2023
by CRC Press
6000 Broken Sound Parkway NW, Suite 300, Boca Raton, FL 33487-2742

and by CRC Press
4 Park Square, Milton Park, Abingdon, Oxon, OX14 4RN

CRC Press is an imprint of Taylor & Francis Group, LLC

Library of Congress Cataloging-in-Publication Data
Names: Ashbourn, Julian, 1952- author.
Title: PKI implementation and infrastructures / Julian Ashbourn.
Description: First edition. | Boca Raton : CRC Press, 2023. | Includes
    bibliographical references and index.
Identifiers: LCCN 2022041809 (print) | LCCN 2022041810 (ebook) | ISBN
    9781032419824 (hbk) | ISBN 9781032419831 (pbk) | ISBN 9781003360674 (ebk)
Subjects: LCSH: Public key infrastructure (Computer security)
Classification: LCC QA76.9.A25 A28247 2023 (print) | LCC QA76.9.A25
    (ebook) | DDC 005.8/24--dc23/eng/20221122
LC record available at https://lccn.loc.gov/2022041809
LC ebook record available at https://lccn.loc.gov/2022041810

ISBN: 978-1-032-41982-4 (hbk)
ISBN: 978-1-032-41983-1 (pbk)
ISBN: 978-1-003-36067-4 (ebk)

DOI: 10.1201/9781003360674

Typeset in Sabon
by SPi Technologies India Pvt Ltd (Straive)

Contents

Introduction
Setting the Scene

An introduction to the world of public key infrastructure (PKI) and IT in general is necessary in order to create an understanding of how we have arrived at the present position and the implications for all those for whom IT is the core of their business which, these days, means practically everybody. The same is, of course, true for government agencies and those in academia. This section might also serve to inform those considering change with respect to the use of cloud-based technologies and associated practices. It also serves as an introduction to the book and its underlying message which, I hope, is understood by all who turn its pages.

INTRODUCTION

For many years, IT was relatively straightforward from an infrastructure perspective. We started off with a client and server model, whereas an organisation, whether it be an academic institution, government agency or commercial enterprise, would store their operational data on a server of some kind. Initially, this would be what we would now call a mainframe computer, with data storage on either tapes (such as those used by professional tape recorders) or hard drives which were, in those days, quite sensitive to movement or shocks, and the ability to use one or more processors. Users would be connected to this central computer via a cabled network, using passive 'dumb' terminals or 'green screens' as they were often called, due to the colour of their text rendering upon a cathode ray tube (CRT) display. Using operating system–specific commands, the user could retrieve information from the central server and post information back to it to be stored within a file directory system.

As time moved on, among the fast-moving changes, there were two significant ones. Firstly, a dichotomy started to appear between large, heavy duty, very powerful computers which became the mainframes previously referred to and smaller, less powerful but more affordable computers, ordinary servers, which were perfectly adequate for many applications in both the commercial and non-commercial sectors, including many university departments. This enabled more people to become familiar with the practical use of a computer, while also increasing the power of mainframes, for those who could afford to use them, such as government agencies. The other significant change was the use of telephone lines in order to extend the network beyond the campus or office. Modems (modulators and demodulators) converted the data into a series of tones which could be passed along a telephone line and reproduced at the other end. Now, it was possible for computers based in academic centres and government agencies to communicate with each other via the telephone network. Of course, the computers concerned had to be able to read the information being passed and be able to practically use it or store it. File systems were therefore developed which would be compatible across different machines.

This method of 'computing' remained the norm for some considerable time, and computers were used mainly for solving problems, undertaking repetitive calculations or operations and storing information in data files. They were administered via dumb terminals by operators who were highly trained in order to use the operating system and programming language in place for their particular system. As time moved on, there was a certain amount of rationalisation with languages such as TPF (Transaction Processing Facility) being used on mainframes and various iterations of UNIX-like operating systems including XENIX which was, for a while, marketed by Microsoft who, in turn, licensed it from AT&T. TPF remains in use today as zTPF as marketed by IBM.

And so, the methodology remained largely the same, with connected networks and variations on operating systems, including special systems for operating networks, complete with their own languages. It all sounds a little complex; however, once installed and set up, these systems were actually relatively straightforward and reliable. Operators quickly learned the various operating system commands and were able to construct databases and various distinct applications, according to whatever use they put the computer to. Academic institutions were primary users of computers, and interactions between computers drove much of the progress in those early days. There was no real problem with computer viruses or even bad code, as most applications were carefully constructed and tested.

Eventually, it was realised that there was a very significant commercial opportunity for supplying both computer hardware, peripherals (such as keyboards and screens) and specialised software such as databases, spreadsheets and early word processors into the commercial world and academia. In the database world, initially, such systems were built from scratch within the operating system until specialised systems such as SABRE appeared. This was developed by IBM for American Airlines (in order that they use IBM computers) and goes back to the 1960s. In the 1970s, systems such as Ingres from UBC and System R from IBM made use of the relational database model, upon which almost everything relied from then on. LANPAR and VisiCalc were pioneers in the spreadsheet world, and there were various attempts at word processors until WordStar really made a big impact, with its easy to use menus and commands.

With all this activity going on, it occurred to many, including IBM, that a smaller 'personal' computer could undertake many traditional office-based tasks and could be used either as a standalone device, or multiples could be networked together in order to construct a much more flexible model for computing. Instead of multiple users having to effectively 'book time' on a mainframe computer, they could each have their own personal computer (PC) and still share data and collaborate on research or business-based activities. While early PCs appeared in the late 1970s, they were clumsy and did not really make much of an impact. However, when IBM launched their PC in August 1981, it really created a revolution in computing. It was well built, reliable and, of course, had the IBM name on it. In fact, the company had earlier launched a portable computer, the 5100 model, in September 1975, but this was more akin to an electronic typewriter with built-in memory and storage. Also, in 1981, Microsoft licensed a disc operating system called 86-DOS from a company named SCP (Seattle Computer Products) and tweaked it a little to operate on the IBM PC, subsequently supplying it to IBM for widespread distribution.

Now, we had a viable computing model which almost any local government agency, academic department or business could use for their own purposes. They could still use mainframes for heavy duty work and the networks created could accommodate both. The PC could effectively be used as a terminal against a mainframe or smaller server, or it could be used as a standalone device. This flexibility revolutionised both the business and enthusiast world. Householders bought PCs in order to use them for simple word processing tasks and to create lists in spreadsheets or databases. Businesses bought PCs and chained them together in small networks, learning network tools such as Novell Netware as they went, enabling workers to collaborate on files and projects. Tools such as Lotus Works for DOS enabled much of the functionality that both personal users and businesses required, with a flat file database, a good word processor and, of course, the Lotus 123 spreadsheet component that was ubiquitous for many years (actually, Lotus Works could facilitate almost everything that people do with computers today). With the advent of Microsoft Windows and the Apple operating system, it all became easier and nicer looking, but we also started to see a myriad of third-party applications that were probably not needed at all. Indeed, with either MS DOS or DR DOS (from Digital Research), enthusiasts and home users could actually do most of what they wanted to do.

And so it went, with new hardware innovations such as faster CPUs (central processing units) and better graphics cards with higher resolutions, and we still had the option to use mainframes or to create networks of PCs and, via modems, to extend the network across telephone lines. However, lurking in the background there was always UNIX and its many variants such as VMS and others. These operating systems sometimes required more specialist hardware, but they were inherently more stable. Furthermore, they had an army of loyal users for whom the Microsoft and Apple worlds were simply not good enough. IBM and Microsoft collaborated for a while on a better operating system called OS2 but, after a while, the two organisations fell out and IBM continued on alone. In fact, OS2 and OS2 Warp as it became known was far superior to MS DOS and Windows, and many business users appreciated its greater stability and superior built-in features such as speech recognition. IBM continued with OS2 until 2005, and many large corporates and government agencies were using it for at least another decade. It was a far superior system to Windows, and this was an early example in IT circles of inferior products holding sway, mainly due to the marketing tactics of the suppliers. It was, unfortunately, an example of what was to come.

Meanwhile, UNIX and its derivatives continued steadily in the background, its users simply ignoring the Microsoft/Apple/IBM debacle and getting on with building solid applications and refining the operating system(s). In academia especially, UNIX had a stronghold as it was stable and promoted the acquisition of computer skills which more closed systems did not. And then, in 1991, a Finnish student named Linus Torvalds decided to create a new operating system kernel which had many of the virtues of UNIX but which could be freely distributed. LINUX was born, and the floodgates opened to a wealth of collaborative development which ensured the provision of a solid, reliable operating system which was freely available to anyone. It prevails today, and many organisations use LINUX to run their servers, even if they are using Microsoft or Apple on the desktop. In fact, there is no reason why they should not use LINUX on the desktop as well as there are many stable distributions from which to choose, the vast majority of which are completely free of cost. This is another example of businesses and government agencies wasting money on IT that they don't need, due to the 'lobbying' activities of suppliers. Actually, you could run any of these enterprises for free with LINUX, while increasing the skills of your IT workforce in the process.

And so, for quite a while, we had a fairly standard way of developing applications for our chosen operating systems. There were development tools such as Microsoft Visual Basic and the excellent Delphi from Borland which had particularly good database connectivity and which shipped with a developer licence for Interbase, one of the very best database tools ever developed (once again, an inferior product won out through more aggressive marketing). With Delphi and Interbase, one could develop any sort of application with Microsoft Windows–based clients. Later on, they would introduce Delphi for LINUX but, by then, scripting languages such as JAVA had also come along and these were platform independent. IBM did much to promote JAVA in the early days. However, with Delphi, one could create properly compiled, self-contained executables that would run on any Windows client and which could connect to any database residing either locally or out on the network. Perfect. With Visual Basic and JAVA, one had to use an additional runtime component which immediately introduced version issues. Certain code would only run with a specific version of the runtime environment. This was a significant backwards step and another example of the poorer option predominating through questionable marketing tactics. With JAVA, you could at least develop code that would run on almost any operating system, providing that the correct version of the runtime JAVA engine was also deployed upon it.

An irony here is that under Borland, the Delphi and associated C++ Builder development environments were years ahead of the competition. Delphi 2 introduced the first 32-bit programming environment. Delphi 3 introduced, among other innovations, the concept of packages, which acted like today's containers, isolating small blocks of code that could be re-used by multiple applications. Thus, with Delphi, you could build your own web server, produce a series of packages to run with it, develop html pages and link things back to a database on your database server, either Interbase or any of the proprietary systems such as Oracle. You could also build your heavy duty background applications and tie everything together neatly, all with just one, small footprint, development tool, using the Object Pascal programming language which was fully object oriented. Anything that can be done today with microservices and containers, you could do with Delphi in the 1990s. Furthermore, it was inexpensive and came with very extensive, printed documentation. If you are thinking that we have surely gone backwards since that time, you are right, we have. Now, we have manifests written in JAML in order to create containers, which we then write code for in a variety of languages, including JAVA, PYTHON, PEARL and many others, then we create an administrative layer around them using Istio or a similar environment, maybe a simplification layer using KNative and we might manage all of this activity via another development layer such as Docker or Ansible and then we might add various automation components, all of which have to reference one another, typically on someone else's infrastructure (the cloud) and then we still need to access our back end data sources. But we could have done all of this with Delphi. Yes, just one simple tool to learn and become proficient with. Borland sold Delphi, and it is still available and being supported by Embarcadero Technologies who, in turn, are owned by Idera Inc. However, it is a slightly different animal now and the elegant simplicity of the earlier versions (up to version 5) is no more. Nevertheless, you may still build almost anything with the current versions of Delphi and for any operating environment.

So, we have complicated, almost beyond belief, the development process for software applications, especially those deployed via the Internet. Users have been duped into a 'cloud first' policy followed by the outsourcing of much of their IT because they simply do not understand it anymore. Even the purveyors of much of the new technology 'stack' do not really understand it. There is a focus upon containers and automation, but no one seems to ask the simple question, why? The focus should be upon real-time operations, not technology. But modern heads of IT (who mostly don't understand it) simply get brainwashed by all the pretence of fast builds and containers and then, usually because they don't really understand it at all, outsource to one of the big four providers (who only understand their version of the technology). But none of these providers understands the operational model, operational requirements and likely operational futures of the companies they are working for. How can they? It is not their operation. The focus should be on the operation, with the technology serving that focus in the most efficient manner. Not the other way around. The new web/cloud-based paradigm does not support that idea.

Underpinning all of this is the subject of this book, PKI (public key infrastructure). In the early days, PKI and the associated use of certificates, including certificate authorities, certificate revocation lists and so on, was generally understood and those organisations that managed their own IT infrastructure had little difficulty with it. If they grew in size, they could utilise a tool such as that offered by Venafi and other suppliers, in order to automatically manage all of their certificates (which have expiry dates) and ensure that all is working as it should. Otherwise, they could simply manage their certificates themselves at the application level via their own application support teams. If they were smart, they would build their own certificate database and build into it the required functionality for their particular operation.

Now, with the modern development model, containers are created and destroyed automatically, links are broken and nobody really knows where everything is. Layers of controlling infrastructure are built upon other layers of controlling infrastructure, using disparate languages and conventions. Managing certificates within such an environment is not impossible but is hugely more troublesome. When certificates expire, or cannot be found due to incorrect addressing, applications break. Things go wrong and operations fail. And it is happening. The large organisation that the author worked for (for 20 years) used to manage its own infrastructure with knowledgeable individuals looking after the applications and operations. Then, they made most of their own staff redundant, brought in consultants, outsourced various IT functions, put a good deal of their infrastructure in the cloud and generally embraced the new model. For 20 years, they had no outages. I read in this week's Sunday paper an article which showed that they had had four major outages within the past few weeks, costing them many tens of millions of pounds, plus a huge amount of customer dissatisfaction. So, why did they do it? Because individuals at director level, no longer know what they are doing. Whether any of this was directly attributable to PKI, I cannot say, but I do know that they are not managing PKI correctly.

The same will be true of many dozens of government agencies, commercial organisations and, probably, a proportion of academia. We will find that many of their key managers and IT staff do not really understand PKI in the first place. Once they go into containers in the cloud, their understanding of the broader picture and how important it is to manage the PKI will be minimal. This is why this introduction has focused upon a brief history of IT and the development model within the IT world before we move on to PKI itself.

SUMMARY

This section has provided a simple history of how the IT world has evolved into what it is today. It has stressed that the current model is not necessarily supporting the needs of business and has, furthermore, become unreliable. It has additionally stressed the importance of a PKI to every such IT model and why this needs to be understood by all those concerned.

Chapter 1

What exactly is a public key infrastructure?

The original concept

People have been sending encrypted messages since as far back as Roman times, if not before. Indeed, it is likely that ancient civilisations, such as the Bronze Age Harappan culture in the Indus Valley and the Neolithic ancient Egyptians in the Nile valley, would have had various ways of encrypting communications. Indeed, recent discoveries have unveiled deliberately obscured or 'encrypted' hieroglyphic writing from ancient Egypt. Their methods must have been particularly interesting. Even before the advent of writing, it is likely that people would use particular spoken phrases in order to indicate particular situations. Children often do the same thing today among their own little groups. It would appear that humanity has an inherent mistrust embedded into the human psyche. Of course, warfare accelerated the idea of secret codes and ciphers. Napoleon used various codes throughout his colourful campaigns and was always tasking his armies to come up with something better. In fact, in France, there were 'grands chiffres' (great ciphers) dating back to the time of Louis XIV. Other countries had their own idea of using codes and, during the Second World War, the Germans used the portable Enigma machines to great effect in order to secure communications, particularly in connection with the U Boats and the devastating affect they had on transatlantic shipping. Fortunately, England had Alan Turing and the team at Bletchley Park who worked on breaking a variety of German codes. England also had the Special Operations Executive, formed in 1940 with volunteers who worked behind enemy lines to cause disruption. These wonderfully brave individuals, many of them women, relied heavily upon codes in order to communicate back to base. The one-time pads that they were using towards the end were often written with invisible ink onto the silk underwear of female agents. They could be read by shining an ultra violet light onto them, provided by a special filter placed over a torch (as an aside, this is why the author's own encryption programme is named SilkPad, in their memory).

DOI: 10.1201/9781003360674-1

With the dawning of the computer age, it quickly became evident that some sort of encryption would be useful in order to protect sensitive information being transmitted across networks. Similarly, information stored on magnetic media could, surely, also be encrypted in order to protect it. Various ideas and applications surfaced and, in the early 1970s, IBM formed a special cryptography group which developed a cipher which quickly became a standard among government agencies and others. It was named the Data Encryption Standard (DES) and was used for many years, until it was eventually broken in 1997. There were variants of it, including triple DES which aimed to be more secure. The primary problem with it, as originally used, was that it was a fixed algorithm. The cipher operated in the same manner whenever it was used. Consequently, it attracted a great deal of attention from those who had reason to break it. Most modern algorithms require a 'seed' in order for them to work to a particular degree or strength. This seed can be a number or a character string; the greater the number of characters, the stronger the seed and the better job the encryption algorithm will make of encrypting the data. Bearing in mind that encryption systems work on the basis of replacing the original characters within a message with alternate characters, the more complex the algorithm and the stronger the seed, the better, as this will produce cipher text (the encrypted message) that is further removed from the original text.

Encryption systems were originally symmetrical, in that the same seed or 'key' was used to both encrypt and decrypt the message. There is nothing wrong with this approach and such systems can work very well indeed. It does mean, however, that the key has to be kept very secret for, if it were to fall into the wrong hands, then encrypted messages could easily be intercepted and deciphered. For centuries, the effective 'key' used to encrypt messages would be a subject of much espionage and intrigue with huge efforts made to discover the secret mechanisms. These consisted, for a very long time, of look-up tables where a letter of the alphabet being used was replaced by another or maybe a set of letters. There were also complicated lists of complete phrases which had special meanings, quite different from what the actual words depicted. These phrase tables could become extremely complex and might be iterated in several volumes of books. Consequently, in earlier times, sending secret messages via cipher text was a complex and time consuming business. The advent of computers made everything much easier and faster, but the underlying principles remained the same. We were using computers to replicate what we had been doing manually with look-up tables and phrase books.

A watershed was reached in 1976 when a research paper written by Whitfield Diffie and Martin Hellman defined a quite different way of using encryption which would become known as the Diffie Hellman key exchange. In this methodology, instead of using the same key both to encrypt and decrypt the message (known as plain text), an asymmetrical pair of keys were used. This key pair was mathematically related in such a way that they must always be used together, but it allowed for one of the pair to be made 'public' while the other could be carefully protected as the 'private' key. It was now possible for a user to give the public key to as many people or organisations as he wished, while keeping the private key safe. Those with the public key could encrypt messages with it using a standard encryption algorithm, but only the holder of the private key could decrypt them. It could also work the other way around. A standard algorithm could also be made publicly available as it was not the algorithm that was important, but the keys used to seed it. The combination of unique key pairs and a readily available algorithm formed the basis to create what has become known as a public key infrastructure or PKI. The algorithm which is most widely used within PKIs is something called AES which stands for 'Advanced Encryption Standard'. The National Institute of Standards and Technology (NIST) began work on AES in 1997, and it was always intended that, while developed primarily for government use, it would be made openly available for widespread use in the interests of securing communication. AES was designed to use a block cipher capable of handling 128 bit blocks with keys of 128, 192 and 256 bits. In order to choose the best algorithm, extensive tests were made with five candidates making the short list. From these, the algorithm eventually chosen was the Rijndael model, submitted by Belgian cryptographers Joan Daemen and Vincent Rijmen. This remains the basis of AES and is widely used throughout the world today. However, it is not quite ubiquitous, and there will be many sophisticated systems in use for special applications (such as SilkPad).

So, now we have a common system for encrypting messages that is proven and open to anyone who wishes to use it. There are many simple applications, such as password managers and email clients, which enable a user to generate a key pair which may be used for encryption and decryption purposes. However, a PKI is a little more sophisticated than this as it describes an entire infrastructure wherein encrypted communication may take place. This is not just in relation to individual messages between human users, but for communication in general, including that between machines. Indeed, the business, governmental and academic worlds rely on machines being able to recognise one another and being able to pass secure communications between them. It has now become even more complex as it is not just individual machines, but virtual machines and containers that require this same level of confidence. Any software-related entity that is connecting to any other such entity, whether it be a web server, a database or simply a file, needs to know that it is connecting to the correct resource. Similarly, that resource needs to know the identity of the service that is connecting to it. There are many criminals out there trying to intercept messages passing between computers and software entities. If they can extract passwords, then they may access all of your business or private data without your knowledge. This is how large organisations have occasionally lost all of their secret customer information, sometimes over an extended period, without being aware of the fact. Of course, computer security and 'cyber' security are more involved than just using a PKI, but the PKI underpins almost all other activities, one way or another, because all transactions require two or more entities to communicate and, for this, they need to ensure the correct identities of all the entities involved. PKI uses the exchange of digital certificates (which will be covered later in this work) in order to verify the identity of the entities involved and encrypt the data which they share between them.

There have been other methodologies, such as Kerberos for example, which have sought to achieve a similar end. In other words, to confirm the identity of the entities involved and to encrypt the data being exchanged, it is promoted as a 'network authentication protocol' and was originally developed by the Massachusetts Institute of Technology. It involves the exchange of tickets via an Authentication Server and Ticket Granting Server in order that a client may connect securely to a server using symmetrical encryption, these days, using the AES encryption algorithm. It works well enough and is a very useful tool. However, a PKI provides a more in-depth service with detailed information about who is connecting to what. In fact, it all started out quite simply as a method for securing communications between two parties. So, if Bob wanted to exchange confidential information with Alice, Bob would generate two cryptographic keys, a private key and a public key. The private key would be held safely within a secure repository on Bob's computer and would never, under any circumstances, be revealed. The public key, however, could be sent out to Alice in order that she might encrypt messages with which it could be sent to Bob and be decrypted only with Bob's private key, via a suitable algorithm. Similarly, Alice could send Bob her public key, with which he could encrypt a message which only she could decrypt with her private key. The public keys would be exchanged via data files called certificates that could be sent via email or another method. They could, for example, be placed on a USB device and handed physically to the recipient in order to ensure that they were correctly delivered. This is a simple example of the original concept of a public key infrastructure. Several commercial email clients implement such an encrypted service using certificates which are exchanged and held within the email client's contact list (Figure 1.1).

One might imagine that if Bob finds he has given his public key to 30 individuals, and they have each given him their public keys, then the situation is starting to become a little complex, especially as certificates have expiry dates and, if attention is not paid to this fact, things can start to go wrong.

Having given a very simple example of a PKI being used between individuals, imagine now a PKI that is used purely between machines, with machine-to-machine authentication and encrypted data passing between them. On a large network, this can become very complex indeed. If we add virtual

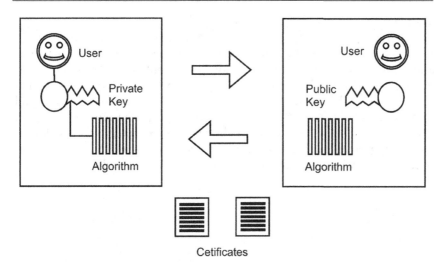

Figure 1.1 A simple PKI example.

machines into this network, the situation becomes more difficult. Now, if we add modern web development models using containers, which themselves need to communicate, the situation can become quite troublesome, especially with respect to the issuance and maintenance of digital certificates.

So, this book will explore all of these areas and, hopefully, find ways in which a PKI may be effectively managed across the very complex space which includes the cloud, virtual machines, containers, conventional on-premise server infrastructure and a wide variety of potential clients. In addition, it will look at Certificate Authorities, Certificate Revocation Lists and other mechanisms which worked well on physical on-premise infrastructure but which become more challenging when that infrastructure reaches into the cloud. Users, whether they be government agencies, academic institutions or commercial entities, should take such matters into consideration before committing to cloud-based infrastructures. Securing your critical data has become ever more important in a world where malicious hackers are everywhere and will not hesitate to exploit any weakness in your infrastructure. They are trying to do this all the time with automated attack systems which are searching for any loopholes in the security of your overall infrastructure (or that of the third parties who are hosting it). This is why, if you are using a PKI, and you should be, it is essential to understand exactly how it is working on your particular infrastructure which, these days, for many organisations, is partly or even wholly cloud based. The days of Bob and Alice have, sadly, long gone. Things have become a tad more complicated since then. However, we shall unravel much of it within this work.

SUMMARY

In this chapter, a brief history of computing in the governmental, academic and commercial fields has been provided, explaining how the situation has developed and what the original thinking was behind PKI. A brief explanation of what a PKI is and how it works in principle has been provided and some of the weaknesses of current software development models have been explored. This has set the scene for the following chapters which will provide greater detail in all of these areas. Suffice it to say that a PKI is a complicated beast which requires very careful consideration and administration.

Chapter 2

How does PKI work?

The Nuts and Bolts of PKI

The example given in the previous chapter was a deliberate simplification intended simply to set the scene. Here, we shall go into the matter in a somewhat greater depth.

Firstly, we must understand that, in the modern world, any human-to-human communication via computers and any machine-to-machine communication via computers is vulnerable. The risks from malicious hackers are very real and, every day, some organisation somewhere experiences a major data breach. It is not always reported as, typically, organisations, and especially, government agencies, do not wish to admit that they have been the subject of an attack and have subsequently lost a great deal of sensitive information. Sometimes, these attacks continue for weeks or even months before they are detected. One might ask how this is possible when many organisations have outsourced the management of their IT, and often their entire IT infrastructure, to one of the giant companies offering such capabilities. But it happens. And then, it happens again. One has to be constantly on the alert in this respect and, unfortunately, mistrust every offered service, including those which claim to provide watertight data security. One must also tread cautiously when adopting new technologies which, quite often, cut across secure methodologies without putting an alternative in place. And then, things get very messy. And so, it will be refreshing to remind ourselves of how a well-implemented public key infrastructure (PKI) should work.

The task is to secure end-to-end communications. We can split this into two fundamental requirements, firstly to authenticate the identity of the user or machine and, secondly, to encrypt the data which are then passed between the two entities. The primary component in this respect is the certificate, which acts to both confirm the identity of the entity, either human or machine, and orchestrate the encryption of the data subsequently sent across the network. To obtain a certificate, a request is made to a registration authority (RA) which serves to confirm the identity of the entity concerned, who then liaises with a certificate authority (CA) who issues the certificate. In the early days of PKI, these two functions were often clearly delineated, and the RA would often authenticate the user manually, via human actions, before advising the CA accordingly. Nowadays, certificate

DOI: 10.1201/9781003360674-2

providers will undertake fairly rudimentary clarification of email addresses and suchlike before selling a certificate, or group of certificates, to the users. And then, there are self-signed certificates, which we shall cover in greater depth later in this work.

From an end users' perspective, most certificates will be those associated with web sites, and in this respect, it is quite easy to examine a web site's certificate by clicking on the little padlock icon adjacent to the search field. Doing so will reveal the basic details of the certificate associated with the web site provider. For example, here are the details of a certificate associated with the Red Hat web site (Figure 2.1).

In this General information tab, the purposes for which the certificate has been issued are specified, together with the name of the entity to which it has been issued. In this case, the web site www.redhat.com. The name of the CA who issued the certificate is given, followed by the validity period of the certificate itself. If one were to click on the 'Issuer Statement' button, the issuer's website will typically be shown with a policy statement or, more

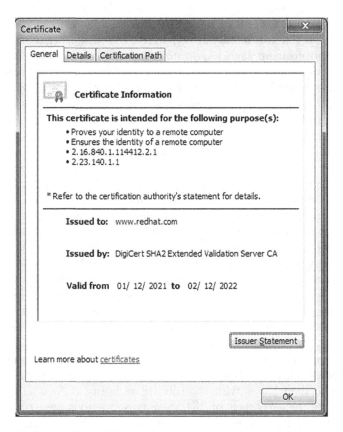

Figure 2.1 Basic certificate information.

typically, a list of policy statements appertaining to certificates issued at different points in time. This information, while interesting enough, will have little practical use for the end user. However, if there is little or nothing displayed here, then that might indicate that something is wrong.

The next tab along displays more detail about the certificate itself and looks as shown in Figure 2.2.

This tab is more interesting and displays the x.509 version number (x.509 is a certificate standard), the serial number, the algorithm used to sign the certificate, the hash algorithm, the certificate issuer, the validity periods, the subject, which is the person or entity to which the certificate has been issued, the public key type and length associated with the certificate, for example, RSA 2048 bits and a whole list of other details associated with the certificate itself. Remember that the certificate contains the public key while the user or entity to whom the certificate was issued retains the private key. The third tab in this dialogue displays the certification path which looks as shown in Figure 2.3.

Figure 2.2 The certificate details tab.

Figure 2.3 The certification path tab.

This tab shows the path by which the certificate was finally issued. In this instance, it is a very simple path; however, occasionally, this path may be quite convoluted with many branches until the final certificate is rendered.

The certificate whose details are shown above is a simple certificate as might be used for web sites. Variations of this simple certificate may be used by individuals in association with email messages, whereby they may use the certificate both to authenticate themselves and also to encrypt messages to those with whom they have exchanged public keys.

The certificates which are used for machine-to-machine authentication and encryption are similar, except the purposes to which they are put, the entities they are issued to and other precise details are, of course, different as we are dealing with identity management for machines, differentiated by IP address. Of course, there may be several IP addresses for a particular server, depending upon both the physical configuration of the device, for example, how many network cards or addresses it is using, and also what software is running on that particular server. Many software applications require certificates in order to communicate with associated applications, either within or beyond the host network. These days, this is further complicated by the reality that so many applications are web based and therefore require data exchange in and out of the host network.

However, let us consider, first of all, how certificates might be used within a typical host network which is built upon an internal architecture, that is, an infrastructure owned by the organisation concerned and hosted within its own premises. Many organisations use the Linux operating system for their main servers, due to its inherent reliability. In order for such servers to communicate securely within a PKI, first of all, they need to know where to look in order to find the appropriate certificates. With Linux, there are well-defined file system hierarchies, but they do vary according to the particular Linux distribution. Many organisations use Red Hat Linux, in which case there is a /etc/pki/tls/certs/ directory for storing certificates and an /etc/pki/tls/private/ directory for storing private keys. On other distributions, such as Debian and Ubuntu, the certificate directory is /etc/ssl/certs/, and for private keys, it is /etc/ssl/private/. There are further variations for distributions such as Open SUSE, Arch and others, but each Linux operating system has a well-defined file location where certificates and keys may be stored.

In Microsoft Windows operating systems, the situation is generally less clear, with certificates stored within the registry under various locations, depending on whether they are user related or machine related. These locations include HKEY_LOCAL_MACHINE root and HKEY_CURRENT_USER root. However, there are both logical and physical locations with certificates stored in both. On Apple MAC OS systems, there is also a differentiation between user and system certificates and the associated stores which are /users/library/keychains/ and /library/keychains/system/. There is also a /system/library/keychains/ which may be used by other applications.

When configuring two computer devices (and applications hosted on those devices) to communicate and pass data between them within a PKI, it will be necessary to identify the appropriate certificates and their locations, in order that they may be referenced and checked before communication may take place. This is undertaken by reference to the appropriate IP address of the device to be communicated with, followed by the path to the certificate for that device or service running on that device and details of the certificate. Bearing in mind that there may be several IP addresses on a particular device and that not all certificates will be in the main directory, some might be within an application's own file system. If this certificate check fails, then an error will be reported. Whether this actually stops the applications from communicating depends upon how they have been built in the first place. Typically, when device A cannot find a valid certificate on device B when it is trying to communicate, then an error message will be reported back to device A and communication will cease. However, this might not always be the case. Sometimes, a warning will be shown with the option to continue or not.

This brings us on to certificate revocation lists (CRLs) which used to be referenced routinely by applications, but this is not necessarily the case within new development methodologies. The idea of a CRL is that, once issued by a reputable CA, should a certificate be cancelled for some reason or otherwise become invalid, its serial number would be added to a published list which, in turn, could be referenced by applications as necessary. Consequently, if a certificate appears on a CRL, even though it appears to be working and is within its date range, an application could refuse to acknowledge it. There are two ways of checking whether a certificate has been revoked. The first is to access the revocation list of the CA who provided the certificate. These are published regularly, and having downloaded the list, it must then be parsed in order to check whether the certificate in question appears on it or not. This requires some programming effort of course, but it should be undertaken for any system using a secure PKI. The second method is known as OCSP checking. OCSP stands for Online Certificate Status Protocol and allows an application to query an OCSP responder which is maintained by the CA. The query effectively asks whether a particular certificate is valid and a response of either 'good', 'revoked' or 'unknown' is returned, allowing the application to react accordingly. OCSP is generally a much faster method of checking whether a certificate is valid. If applications do not check either published CRLs or undertake real-time OCSP checks, then they cannot have complete confidence in a given certificate.

Within a network, an organisation can easily create its own CRL and publish it in a known location. This is useful for large organisations who may be running thousands of servers. Similarly, for government agencies or academic institutions, it makes sense to publish an organisation-specific CRL in order that untrusted certificates will not be used. Such a CRL may be very simple, and operating systems usually include tools to help manage them (Figure 2.4).

There is some question as to how often CRLs are really being checked or, in some cases, whether they are being checked at all. In addition, there have been some issues with CRLs simply becoming too large to manage effectively and also with the standard OCSP checks as they are open to particular types of attacks due to the original protocols being used. In response to this, a system known as OCSP Stapling has been introduced which greatly improves privacy and security. This enables a web service to send a signed response from the OCSP check with information about the current certificate as part of the Transport Layer Security (TLS) handshake. The client can verify the OCSP response as it is signed by the CA and thus be confident that the certificate has not been revoked. This is also more efficient from a processing perspective.

When everything is configured properly, a PKI enables the secure use of machine-to-machine connections over a network and is key to secure web services and applications. It is also an integral part of the Internet, and web

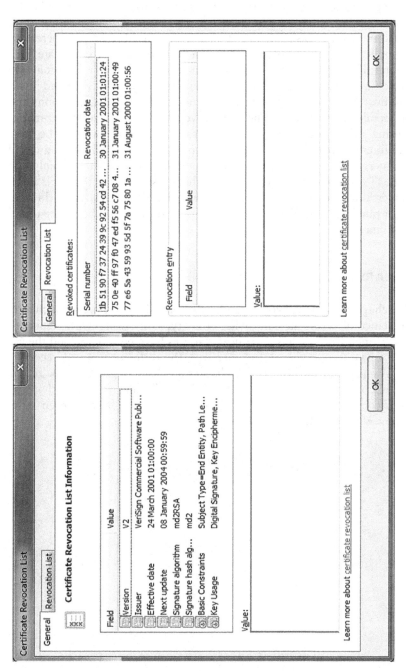

Figures 2.4 A simple revocation list example.

browsers have inherent capabilities to check the certificates of web servers. However, the larger scenario can become quite complicated at the organisation level. Someone needs to be responsible for ensuring that certificates are renewed in a timely fashion and, of course, they need to know where they are. Applications are available with which to manage a corporate PKI, including the discovery of certificates which may have been forgotten and the automatic renewal of all certificates. This is entirely practical and possible as most of the CAs can connect automatically to such applications and work seemlessly with them. The alternative is to manage everything manually, using a database of known certificates, but this approach can be quite labour intensive once the server estate starts growing. In addition, in a world where mergers and acquisitions are commonplace, one might suddenly find that the IT estate has doubled in size, in which case, merging two PKIs is not an undertaking for the faint-hearted, as we shall discover later. In this scenario, a purpose-built PKI management application would be a very useful thing to have.

SUMMARY

In this chapter, the inner workings of a PKI have been examined, including the issuance of certificates and where they typically reside with respect to different operating systems. Certificate failures have been noted and the use of CRLs has been explored, together with the different ways of accessing them. The primary purpose of this chapter has been to acquaint the reader with the component parts of a PKI and instil the understanding that it is quite a complicated scenario. The reality of this will become even more apparent within forthcoming chapters.

Chapter 3

What are the primary applications for a PKI?

How applications are changing

The original intention of public key infrastructure (PKI) was to improve upon the symmetrical encryption that had been in use between data entities. There was nothing particularly wrong with symmetrical encryption when implemented properly, but it did mean that, should the key or pass phrase be compromised and the algorithm guessed, then any messages or information thus encrypted could be easily decrypted by whoever had the key. There were ways in which this could be made safer. For example, by ensuring that every single data exchange was encrypted slightly differently. Also, a non-standard encryption algorithm could be used which might work in a completely different way to the norm. And those using such applications could devise ways of using them which would be hard to guess. The SilkPad application takes advantage of all of these techniques (and, by the way, has never been defeated). However, for large organisations and individuals alike, using a symmetrical system safely required some careful thinking, planning and execution.

With an asymmetrical system, a greater range of possibilities arose, especially when separating the encryption algorithm from the keys being used to seed it. In the Diffie-Hellman research paper proposing asymmetrical encryption, it was realised that with sensible use of the keys, the actual algorithm used need not be kept secret but, indeed, could actually be published for all to use. At the time the Data Encryption Standard (DES) was considered adequate, but this was eventually retired in favour of Advanced Encryption Standard (AES) using the Rijndael algorithm with asymmetrical keys of a particular length. For most, the idea of encryption still related to the safe sending of messages between two individuals. If Bob and Alice wished to embrace PKI, they would both generate a pair of keys, one private key and one public key, and obtain a certificate via a registration authority (RA)and a certificate authority (CA). Each of them would keep their private key safe, but they would exchange their public keys. Now, Bob could use Alice's public key to encrypt a message to her which only she could decrypt with her private key, and Alice could use Bob's public key to encrypt a message that only Bob could decrypt with his private key. This was facilitated by the use of certificates which could easily be exchanged via email or even

DOI: 10.1201/9781003360674-3

physically on a floppy disc. Once the concept had been grasped, this was all quite easy to do. However, grasping the concept proved quite hard for many, and it is still quite rare for private individuals to use certificates in order to secure email traffic. With the advent of mobile phones and so-called smart phones, there are services who offer end-to-end message encryption, but questions have arisen as to just how safe these systems are as the encryption is, after all, in someone else's hands. It might be better to use conventional email with certificates, and these days, almost all email clients offer the capability to do so.

If only one party has a certificate, it is still possible to sign messages with it, thereby authenticating the identity of the sender. In which case, recipients will get a message something as shown in Figure 3.1.

This is easily achieved with modern email clients who make such operations as simple as clicking on a button (Figure 3.2).

And so, it is worth obtaining a simple 'email' certificate and encouraging those with whom you regularly communicate to do the same. When you first send them a signed message, they will also get your public key, which they may store in their address book. Now, they may encrypt messages which they send to you, using this key within their usual email client. As more individuals within a particular social circle do this, they will effectively create their own decentralised PKI, at least for the exchange of data via email. This is a simple and worthwhile thing to do and echoes the original intentions for what became known as PKI. Furthermore, anyone can do so, and there are some certificate authorities offering free email certificates for private use. Installing them is straightforward in most cases with facilities to do so an inherent part of almost every popular email client. In addition, such an activity encourages the thinking around security and privacy, which is never a bad thing, both from a personal and organisational perspective.

The exchange of email messages remains, therefore, a valid use of certificates and an effective PKI, even though it is effectively decentralised and in

Security Help
Digitally Signed Message

This message has been digitally signed by the sender.

Signed email from others allows you to verify the authenticity of a message -- that the message is from the supposed sender and that it has not been tampered with during transit. Signed mail messages are designated with the signed mail icon.

Any problems with a signed message will be described in a Security Warning which may follow this one. If there are problems, you should consider that the message was tampered with or was not from the supposed sender.

☐ Don't show me this Help screen again.

Continue

Figure 3.1 A message confirming the identity of the sender as it has been signed.

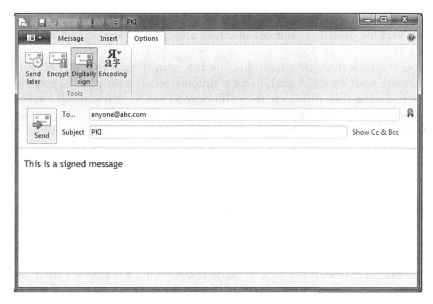

Figure 3.2 A typical email client providing certificate services.

the hands of many users, each of whom must be responsible for the ongoing management of their particular certificate and associated credentials. When extrapolated to the organisational level, personal certificates may be kept in a corporate directory, together with other user-related information, and managed effectively from there. It is interesting how many organisations which have a PKI do not use it to protect email messages, and yet, this is a potential source of security leaks. If we are protecting machine-to-machine communications, we may as well do the same for humans.

Machine-to-machine identification within the same network is another application which relies upon certificates and keys. If it is within your own network, i.e., within the same organisation, it is feasible to use self-signed certificates, in which case it will be necessary to establish your own CA on a dedicated server somewhere on your network. On typical Linux distributions, you can do this by creating a path called 'easy-rsa' into which you create a 'vars' file, something like this:

```
~/easy-rsa/vars
set_var EASYRSA_REQ_COUNTRY    "UK"
set_var EASYRSA_REQ_PROVINCE   "Derbyshire"
set_var EASYRSA_REQ_CITY       "Matlock"
set_var EASYRSA_REQ_ORG        "Deckers"
set_var EASYRSA_REQ_EMAIL      "admin@deckers.com"
set_var EASYRSA_REQ_OU         "Community"
set_var EASYRSA_ALGO           "ec"
set_var EASYRSA_DIGEST         "sha512"
```

after which you can create the CA with the command '/easyrsa build-ca'. The vars file describes your organisation and includes the sort of information that would be found in commercially supplied certificates. Actually, there is a little more to it than this, but the main thing is that it is possible to create your own CA and, using a suitably secure pass phrase, generate key pairs and then distribute the public key to wherever it is needed across the network. Doing things manually like this may be a good approach within your own network as it will embed a PKI philosophy within the organisation. Furthermore, if you have a large number of servers and clients, it would represent an economical approach, although it must be undertaken according to a strict rigour with regard to expiry dates. However, if you are accessing servers on another network and others are accessing your network, then you really need to use certificates bought from an external, specialist CA. These need to be placed in the appropriate certificate stores within your network and updated when necessary. This organisation-to-organisation approach to machine identification is a major use of PKI and, of course, it needs to be undertaken with some care as, often, if a certificate expires or is unrecognised, it may mean that a particular service is denied. So, machine-to-machine identification has really taken over as the main application for PKI and sits behind most governmental, commercial and academic activities, wherein trust is essential when dealing with partners across networks. Bob and Alice have missed the boat slightly in this respect.

And, of course, we now live in a world which is dominated by the Internet, with almost everything being done on-line or relying on some web-centric service or other. Consequently, there are many millions of browsers accessing web services and applications on web servers which may even be situated in other countries. This makes machine identity even more important, together with the encryption of data passing across unknown networks in order to interact with web services and applications. Fortunately, this is reasonably well understood and web servers exchange information with web browsers via encrypted links using certificates. This is the basis of the https protocol which is now used almost universally for any website exchanging sensitive data such as payments and financial information. It requires sites to utilise SSL/TLS (Secure Sockets Layer or more recently Transport Layer Security) which, in turn, requires the use of certificates. It is easy to check the certificate for a given web site by clicking on the little padlock icon to the left of the search bar. There you should find independently verified details of the organisation hosting that particular web site. Undoubtedly, the Internet represents the most prolific use of PKI, although it is in the hands of a great many people and many users will simply not understand whether their transaction is sufficiently protected or not. In this respect, it makes sense to use a secure browser to protect against eavesdropping and other attempts to steal information. There are just a few of them out there that are good in this respect while many which claim to be secure are not really, as they are continuously sending data back to the browser provider, who then sells it on. However, this is another security related issue outside the scope of this book.

And now, we have another, very important use of PKI and that relates to applications which are built for deployment on the web. The development methodology for these applications has changed significantly in recent years, and now, there is a trend for developing small sections of code in 'containers' and then deploying these, almost like virtual machines, usually in the cloud. This will be covered later in this work but, suffice it to say, that there is a real need for machine identity management in this context. Furthermore, it is not clear that this requirement is being adequately met at the present time. There are reasons for this which will be explained later.

These are the primary applications for PKI. There are a number of other uses to which certificates may be put, especially within industry. For example, we now have certificates on board for every commercial aircraft (and no doubt military aircraft as well), and there will be many processes in automated manufacturing where certificates may be required. In the case of aircraft, there may or may not be a network involved depending on local facilities. It is possible to use a wireless network but it might equally be the case of an engineer going on board with a laptop computer and connecting directly to the on-board computers, the connection being verified by valid certificates issued by a trusted CA. These specialist applications would do well to use a proper PKI management system which guarantees the timely updating of certificates while giving the organisation a centralised view of their certificate estate. An application may be defined simply as any instance in which two or more devices need to communicate with each other over a network, whether trusted or untrusted. In such a scenario, certificates enable each entity to identify itself according to a known and trusted methodology which utilises CAs, unique key pairs and a trusted algorithm with which to encrypt and decrypt data. When deployed as designed, this methodology provides a high level of trust which enables business-related transactions to be undertaken over an unknown and untrusted network. Consequently, every organisation should have a well-designed PKI.

These days, the architectural design of such a PKI should take into account the new ways in which applications are being built, around microservices and containers, and may, consequently, become rather more complex than has hitherto been the case. The primary applications remain the same, but the way of addressing them has become much more complex. In most cases, some sort of automated certificate management system will be appropriate. In addition, personnel must be trained, both in general terms and in connection with whatever system is used to manage certificates, and competence created within the organisation accordingly.

SUMMARY

In this chapter, the primary uses for a PKI have been examined together with a little more insight as to how the methodology may be used practically. It is important to understand that PKI is not just one, closed system, but more of a way of doing things that may be extrapolated to many applications. Anywhere where machine identity is important represents a possible application of a PKI. The PKI itself is really just a structure. The application is the process of applying that structure to a particular task, of which there may be a great number within a typical organisation. Certainly, every organisation and every user of the Internet is already exposed to a PKI. The question is how well they understand it and, consequently, manage it.

Chapter 4

What exactly is a digital certificate?

The contents of a certificate

Put simply, a digital certificate is a file. Within this file, certain details about either an individual or an organisation are to be found. This information is usually verified by a third party, the certificate authority (CA). Once the CA has verified that the individual or organisation really does exist, then they are happy to issue a digital certificate containing the appropriate details. Certificates are also commonly issued for web sites, using the same rigour of a CA to verify that they are what they appear to be. This should go a long way to preventing duplicate sites springing up. If you are ever unsure that a web site is genuine, check the details of its digital certificate. It is not an absolute guarantee, but it is a good measure of authenticity, assuming that the contents of the certificate make sense and align with the organisation being presented.

The most commonly used certificates adhere to a standard named x.509. This standard was developed by the International Telecommunication Union (ITU) which is itself an agency of the United Nations. An x.509 compliant certificate binds an identity to a public key via a digital signature. There are various algorithms used for the digital signature, just as there are various algorithms used for data encryption, which is itself facilitated by certificates and keys. The final certificate includes the public key of the organisation or individual to whom it was issued. This key may be used by third parties to encrypt data being sent back to the host. The x.509 standard defines various fields which should be included in the certificate. These are as follows:

- Certificate
- Version Number
- Serial Number
- Signature Algorithm ID
- Issuer Name
- Validity Period
- Not Before
- Not After

- Subject Name
- Subject Public Key Info

DOI: 10.1201/9781003360674-4

- Public Key Algorithm
- Subject Public Key

- Issuer Unique Identifier (optional)
- Subject Unique Identifier (optional)
- Extensions (optional)
- ...

- Certificate Signature Algorithm
- Certificate Signature

Not all certificates will include all of this information as some fields are optional, but most should be fully populated as appropriate. All fields that are used must be processed by those applications that reference the certificate. A populated certificate may appear as quite a large file, such as that shown below:

```
Certificate:
  Data:
    Version: 3 (0x2)
    Serial Number:
      03:04:54:08:f9:ff:10:92:e1:69:fe:49:8f:78:d3:6d:dc:47
    Signature Algorithm: sha256WithRSAEncryption
    Issuer: C = DE, O = Let's Encrypt, CN = R3
    Validity
      Not Before: Jul 15 08:01:49 2021 GMT
      Not After : Oct 13 08:01:48 2021 GMT
    Subject: CN = *.mysite.org
    Subject Public Key Info:
      Public Key Algorithm: id-ecPublicKey
        Public Key: (256 bit)
        pub:
          04:a5:9a:47:b2:d3:fc:a7:df:de:f6:cb:45:62:0a:
          d3:c1:a7:38:de:20:bd:d7:10:7d:58:73:de:8d:a1:
          99:70:0c:dd:ab:91:3f:0e:83:97:1b:4f:a2:99:f3:
          f8:30:73:ef:da:be:91:25:18:7a:d6:da:bf:e5:e9:
          72:a3:41:31:7a
        ASN1 OID: prime256v1
        NIST CURVE: P-256
    X509v3 extensions:
      X509v3 Key Usage: critical
        Digital Signature
      X509v3 Extended Key Usage:
        TLS Web Server Authentication, TLS Web Client
        Authentication
      X509v3 Basic Constraints: critical
        CA:FALSE
      X509v3 Subject Key Identifier:
        08:0E:29:26:07:E9:B4:5B:63:2D:86:5D:F6:E2:5A:8C:CD:
        6A:D0:A7
```

```
X509v3 Authority Key Identifier:
   keyid:14:2E:B3:14:B7:58:56:CB:AE:54:09:40:E6:1F:AF:
   9D:8B:14:C2:C6

Authority Information Access:
 OCSP - URI:http://r3.o.lencr.org
 CA Issuers - URI:http://r3.i.lencr.org/

X509v3 Subject Alternative Name:
   DNS:*.mysite.org, DNS:*.mydata.org, DNS:*.mymedia.
   org, DNS:mycontent.org
X509v3 Certificate Policies:
   Policy: 2.23.140.1.2.1
   Policy: 1.3.6.1.4.1.44947.1.1.1
     CPS: http://cps.letsencrypt.org

CT Precertificate SCTs:
   Signed Certificate Timestamp:
     Version : v1 (0x0)
     Log ID : F6:5C:93:2F:D1:77:30:26:14:52:13:08:30:9
     4:56:8E:
       E3:4D:13:13:31:BF:DF:0C:2F:24:0B:CB:4E:F1:64:E3
     Timestamp : Jul 25 09:01:49.274 2020 GMT
     Extensions: none
     Signature : ecdsa-with-SHA256
       30:46:02:21:00:81:0F:F3:F1:BC:A2:AD:B3:7B:FD:C2:
       A6:6A:1B:4C:1F:35:18:7B:3F:18:F6:43:29:46:F6:C2:
       DD:15:63:C1:5D:02:21:00:CF:E0:3F:3D:E7:4A:37:C6:
       CD:E5:BC:CD:93:FE:9C:F1:F7:EA:01:2D:97:DA:C2:74:
       A6:30:37:57:F0:32:82:73
   Signed Certificate Timestamp:
     Version : v1 (0x0)
     Log ID : 6F:51:72:AC:35:F0:33:19:D8:99:00:A4:54:15
     :FF:73:
       15:1C:11:D9:02:C1:00:26:06:8D:B2:08:9A:37:D9:13
     Timestamp : Jul 15 09:01:50.105 2021 GMT
     Extensions: none
     Signature: ecdsa-with-SHA256
       30:42:02:24:31:BC:8F:6A:BA:FA:AC:0B:5B:4C:3F:C8:
       C2:AB:EA:2B:60:DE:A8:AB:44:71:E5:43:6A:E0:0A:24:
       32:49:7F:33:02:25:11:AF:F7:65:43:81:07:C7:FB:B6:
       89:55:0B:74:58:61:76:FB:62:FF:F4:C9:D0:C6:A7:43:
       63:98:4C:F5:4C:7E
Signature Algorithm: sha256WithRSAEncryption
   8e:f4:d1:85:9c:96:e8:63:d0:38:fd:7a:cc:d5:ad:b2:06:b4:
   4a:cf:3d:5a:b9:c2:28:3d:58:57:8a:55:44:ec:91:d3:ca:4f:
   ec:97:c0:10:73:75:43:5c:74:be:7e:2a:89:d8:fa:86:2f:8d:
   d3:57:99:67:3a:f6:28:6c:d1:26:29:ce:cf:7e:96:bd:34:0e:
   86:98:b3:0b:2e:23:dc:5b:46:77:32:a7:d9:b1:e6:de:e9:9a:
   2b:5d:03:f2:e0:07:12:03:d9:03:a8:ef:47:60:16:55:2a:32:
```

```
53:c9:b3:4c:54:99:e0:98:d6:5f:1a:94:1c:6c:c5:e9:13:f7:
03:c7:b6:b5:dd:d8:2b:b5:b7:2e:ba:cb:0b:2d:be:50:c6:85:
0d:22:46:5e:e6:5f:b7:d4:86:45:d8:a4:bf:80:18:6e:46:96:
d1:76:93:f5:40:e2:15:18:be:e0:cb:5f:cd:d0:4f:fa:ca:76:
68:ba:94:c4:1d:1a:0e:3d:3b:ef:ed:1e:29:38:1d:22:bb:8b:
96:71:55:b7:e4:8b:31:34:ec:63:09:e9:1c:d8:2f:f8:9a:b7:
78:dc:33:c9:4e:84:82:03:0b:c5:52:af:9e:b0:6a:dc:fe:9e:
89:2f:17:40:69:74:71:65:37:38:b4:28:23:01:01:81:19:23:
23:cd:75:a0
```

As we can see, that is quite a lot of information, but it can be read very quickly by even a basic computer. A human reader may easily understand it, although they don't really need the precise detail of things like the signature algorithm. Fortunately, it is much easier to check the details of a certificate as most operating systems have a certificate viewer application as do most web browsers.

In Figure 4.1 above, we can see that this particular certificate has been provided for the purpose of authenticating the identity of both me as a user

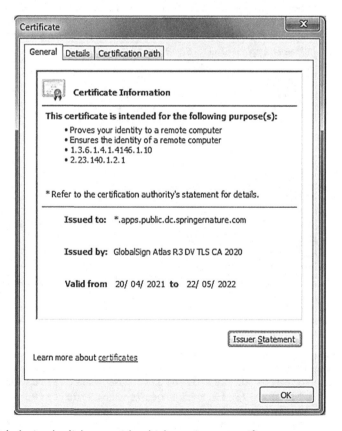

Figure 4.1 A simple dialogue with which to view a certificate.

(in fact, my computer) and that of a remote computer, in this case, the web server delivering the on-line content. We can see that it has been issued to Springer Nature under the domain name of.apps.public.dc.springernature. com and that it has been issued by GlobalSign who are a popular CA. We may further check the validity period and, as I write this, the certificate remains in date. The other tabs on this dialogue enable us to check the details, which will reveal a great deal more about the certificate, including much of the information on the previous page and also the certification path which tells us that the certificate originated at the GlobalSign root level, went through the GlobalSign issuing process and finally arrived at Springer Nature. In some cases, the certification path might be more elaborate, but this is a simple web certificate, the details of which are well established, as is the issuance process. Things might become a little more complicated with a certificate for a very specific and complex use.

Having been issued, certificates will be stored in the expected locations, depending upon whether the device is UNIX/Linux, Apple Mac or Windows based, or indeed, it may be residing on a mainframe computer running z/OS or similar. Or it may be application specific and running within the file system of the application concerned, such as the db2/ssl_ keystore within an IBM DB2 database system. Many applications maintain their own keystores and other applications will need to reference them directly. This is all part of application deployment and management as undertaken by competent IT departments. When installing a new application, it is necessary to understand what other applications or services it will connect to and where the relevant certificates reside. As might be imagined, this can become quite complicated with respect to a large IT estate, which is why a dedicated certificate management system is usually a good idea, provided of course, that it is actually used. This will usually entail a number of individuals being specifically trained and certified in the use of the tool (Figure 4.2).

From the above, it will be seen that managing a PKI is not a small undertaking. Certificates themselves can be tricky if attention is not paid to them. In particular, their precise location and, of course, their expiry dates. When IT infrastructure grows, or is otherwise altered, certificates require particular attention. They may be just little text files, but they are little text files which enable or disable the correct operation of IT systems. In a typical government agency, academic institution or commercial operation, there may be thousands or even hundreds of thousands of them. A single certificate, in the wrong place, could bring a particular operation or task to a standstill and support staff may not understand why this has occurred. Consequently, they are worthy of our best attention.

Extrapolating this organisational model to the Internet places things on an altogether different scale, and while things mostly work well enough, via https and Transport Layer Security (TLS), it is useful to use a secure browser and to periodically check the certificates of important sites such as banking

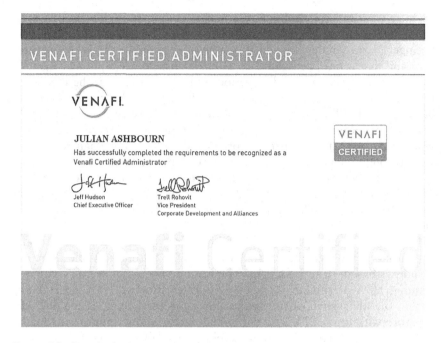

Figure 4.2 Certified administration of tools is a good approach.

sites or any retail related sites where financial transactions may occur. Certificates cannot guarantee against fraud, but they do ensure that there is a level of trust in place and that the sites function as intended. It is worth getting to know them intimately and understanding how they work within the broader scheme of things. Even private individuals should do this. Furthermore, if the IT has been outsourced within an organisation, then it would be wise to obtain a complete map of all the certificates being used on the system. If the company to which it has been outsourced cannot provide this, then there is something gravely wrong and steps should be taken to extricate oneself from such a position.

SUMMARY

In this chapter, we have explained what a certificate is and what it consists of, giving one or two examples as appropriate. We have already covered the issuing process, and we have here additionally stressed the importance of certificates to the broader operation, as so much of what we do relies upon them. Managing certificates should therefore be high on the agenda of any IT operation and this has also been stressed.

Chapter 5

What about encryption?

How a public key infrastructure is used for encryption

Data encryption has been around for a long time. There is some evidence that the ancient Egyptians used a system of symbol replacement, much like we use character replacement today. In which case, it is also likely that the Sumerians, Hittites and Harappans, among others, may equally have been doing something along these lines. By the time we get to the Romans, the concept was well established. Since then, there have been a wealth of different ideas, from complicated character or whole word replacement, to phrase books and look-up tables where completely different phrases would be used to convey the meaning of a given message. Mostly, these were used for military purposes or for secrecy and espionage among royalty and governments. However, there were always those who developed systems out of curiosity, some of which were adopted and sometimes adapted by governments. Nearly all of them work on the principle of replacing the original characters (plain text) with alternative characters and symbols (cipher text) and are therefore irrevocably aligned with the character set being used which, itself, may vary across written languages.

In modern history, one of the most significant steps forward for encryption systems came in 1918 when German engineer Arthur Scherbius invented the Enigma machine, a mechanical device which employed a series of rotors which used a complex coding mechanism in order to replace one character with another. Perhaps, one of the most significant points of the Enigma was the fact that it could be 'seeded' with a special group of characters before encryption or decryption began. This meant that the seed could be changed on a daily basis, making it very difficult for anyone attempting to break the code. Unbeknown to the Germans, Polish code breakers had anticipated what was going on and had built a machine, affectionately known as the 'bombe' in order to guess the German ciphers. This was fine until the Germans added more rotors to their Enigma machines, making it more difficult to break the code. However, by this time, and with the Second World War looming, the Polish engineers had shared their achievements with their British and French allies, and at Bletchley Park in England, Alan Turing

DOI: 10.1201/9781003360674-5

soon developed a more sophisticated 'bombe' with help from the British Tabulating Machine Company and engineer Harold Keen. This device may be considered the first proper, large-scale computer, and it was instrumental in breaking the German naval codes and, no doubt, shortening the war.

After the war, particularly in the 1970s, there was much activity with regard to ciphers and encryption as it was obvious that computers were going to play a large part in the modern world and that encryption was going to play a large part in computing. Hence, the introduction of Data Encryption Standard (DES), Blowfish and many other algorithms. Interestingly, these all worked on the same ideas that had inspired the original Enigma machine and, indeed, encryption systems for hundreds of years prior to that. That is the process of replacing one character with another (or sometimes one phrase with another). We can try this for ourselves in a very simple manner. Let's take the letters A,E,I,O,U and replace them in a table as follows:

a	E	i	o	u
f	H	t	k	s

Now, let us construct a simple sentence as follows:

'This is a very interesting book published by'.

Now, let us substitute the characters from our table:

'Thts ts f vhry tnthrhsttng bkkk psbltshhd by fsprhss'.

Let us further complicate things by eliminating the spaces between words:

'Thtstsfvhrytnthrhsttngbkkkpsbltshhdbyfsprhss'.

The result is a text string which, at first sight, seems rather meaningless. However, a good cryptographer would probably decipher that string fairly easily, firstly by looking for the presence of repeating characters and then by substituting the most regularly used characters in written text. However, we only changed five characters. Imagine if we had changed every character in the alphabet, as well as the numerals 0 to 9. Then, we would have a cipher which was much stronger and much harder to break. Nevertheless, good code breakers are remarkably proficient at breaking codes. During the Second World War, the Special Operations Executive in London employed a few rooms full of bright young ladies who were, effectively, human computers. Each group was given part of an encoded message, and sooner or later, they would break the code, with nothing more than a pencil and paper, together, of course, with their intuition and the training that they had received. Their particular gift to humanity is incalculable, and they should be remembered with great affection and pride.

Modern encryption systems are more sophisticated but still work in more or less the same way. The key, as provided by the public key within a certificate, acts as a seed with which to seed a known algorithm, such as the Advanced Encryption Standard (AES) Rijndael algorithm. The length of the key is important as keys of longer lengths provide a more complicated seed to the algorithm. Consequently, a 512-bit key will typically provide stronger encryption than a 256-bit key. A 1024-bit key is better still as it will provide greater 'scrambling' within the same algorithm.

An alternative to using keys is to use pass phrases. These have the advantage of being easy to remember and can be quite long, providing the equivalent of a very large key indeed. They may also be easily changed from one day to another according to an agreed set of rules. For example, two individuals using a symmetrical encryption system with pass phrases to seed an unknown algorithm might agree to use the first sentence of consecutive chapters from a particular edition of a particular book by Charles Dickens. This could work quite well in practice. However, in times of espionage and warfare, being easy to remember is not necessarily a good thing, neither is a system of phrases which, after discovering one of them, might be easily guessed. With a public key infrastructure (PKI) and strong key lengths, no one will be able to remember the key, even if they have seen it in text form.

Encryption itself is a fascinating subject (the author has written several algorithms and produced three or more systems, purely as a challenge). The current PKI methodology is fine and well suited to the computer age, provided it is used correctly. However, that does not preclude the use of other methodologies for specific applications, especially when something quite simple to use is required, perhaps, for example for agents to use in the field. Let us take our same phrase of 'This is a very interesting book published by and type it into the SilkPad application. What we get is shown in Figure 5.1.

I would defy anyone to decipher this particular block of cipher text and arrive at the same sentence. Indeed, SilkPad has been around for more than 20 years and no one has ever broken SilkPad-encoded cipher text, even though prizes have been offered and cipher text has been sent to intelligence agencies all over the world. One can see immediately that the cipher text is a good deal longer than the plain text. Obviously, there is something more than a simple character replacement taking place here. In fact, a single character of plain text may be represented by multiple characters of cipher text, the exact number changing on a dynamic basis according to a particular set of rules. This is not a new approach: the Arabs came up with something similar around a.d. 900 and were very advanced in mathematics generally

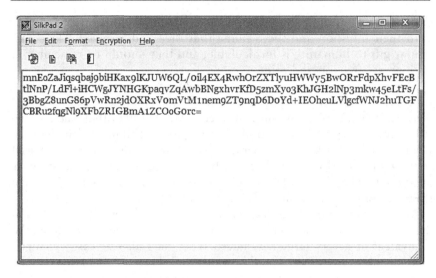

SilkPad 2

File   Edit   Format   Encryption   Help

mnEoZaJiqsqbaj9biHKax9lKJUW6QL/oil4EX4RwhOrZXTlyuHWWy5BwORrFdpXhvFEcB
tlNnP/LdFl+iHCWgJYNHGKpaqvZqAwbBNgxhvrKfD5zmXyo3KhJGH2lNp3mkw45eLtFs/
3BbgZ8unG86pVwRn2jdOXRxVomVtM1nem9ZT9nqD6DoYd+IEOhcuLVlgcfWNJ2huTGF
CBRu2fqgNl9XFbZRIGBmA1ZCOoGorc=

Figure 5.1 An encrypted sentence in SilkPad.

at that time. Indeed, the word 'algebra' comes from the same source. But SilkPad is behind the scenes doing something unique with respect to encryption algorithms, and this is why the created cipher text cannot be broken. Consequently, it is a perfect system for any two (or more) operators to use when they need something simple, which does not require any third-party infrastructure. In addition, SilkPad runs from a single executable file of just 660 kB in size and may be used from a Universal Serial Bus (USB) stick with no dependencies from the host device. Furthermore, it may use either pass phrases or a key of some kind to seed the algorithm, and these are easily stored within the application as may be seen below (Figure 5.2).

The dialogue shown below illustrates how easy it is to set a pass phrase within SilkPad. The user, having set the pass phrase, simply types in the message and presses the encrypt button. The cipher text may then be sent in an email message or by other means to the recipient who simply uses the same pass phrase and presses the decrypt key to return the plain text. It is a very simple and elegant system, built in order to demonstrate the principles of encryption, while offering a challenge to code breakers.

The AES algorithm used within most PKI systems may be thought of as an equivalent to the SilkPad internal algorithm, and the public keys used within certificates may be thought of as the pass phrases used within SilkPad in order to seed the algorithm. This somewhat lengthy explanation has served to illustrate what happens with PKI encryption; however, there is still the question of how it happens. With many applications, such as the Internet, it happens more or less automatically. If those creating web servers and web sites are using the https protocol with Transport Layer Security (TLS), then certificates will automatically be exchanged and data encrypted as it travels

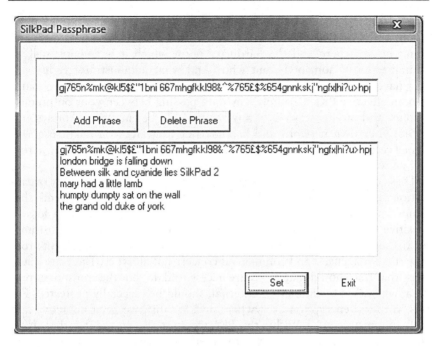

Figure 5.2 Setting a pass phrase in SilkPad.

to and from the browser. With other applications, it may require user intervention. For example, most email clients provide options for encryption, but the user has to make a choice and take a deliberate action to encrypt the message and that, of course, requires that he has the public key of the other party. This will usually be stored in the address book associated with the email client.

But what about machine-to-machine encryption? This will need to be specifically coded for as each device will need to know where to get the certificate of the other and vice versa, then they will need to take an action to encrypt the data passing between them. If they use the appropriate protocols, then this will happen. And this is the second important function of a PKI, the first being to authenticate users or machines and the second being to encrypt and decrypt the data passing between them. Within a large IT estate, this picture can become quite complicated, especially when dealing with a number of third parties. This is becoming increasingly prevalent as suppliers are increasingly providing Software as a Service (SAAS) and, very often, the software involved remains on-line. This means that sensitive data is passing back and forth across an untrusted network (the Internet). Organisations should think very carefully before opting to use such services. First of all, they have no idea from where the service is actually being hosted. It could be, quite literally, anywhere in the world. Secondly, they have no idea who is administering the software and what access they might have to user's data. The same goes for anything that is either placed or hosted in the cloud. The actual service, even if it is your own custom developed software, could be anywhere and the hardware upon which it is running will be administered by somebody, but who? And what administrator rights will they have? Questions such as these make it all the more important to maintain an effective PKI. Certainly, any data passing between your on-premise systems and on-line services of any kind should be encrypted. For systems within your own network and behind your firewalls, you might use self-signed certificates, but it is still a good idea to encrypt all data passing across any network and between any machines.

These days, industrial and political espionage is very real and any organisation has to be especially careful with its precious data. It seems that almost every day we hear about some major data breach and the loss of sensitive information. Often, this information is in the form of customer details, not just from banks (although they are a prime target) but from government agencies and commercial concerns of all types. There are many steps that one should take to secure access to data, but the transmission of data, whether it be internal or external, should be especially protected. For this, we need encryption everywhere and for this, we need an active and well-administered PKI. Within this PKI, we must also ensure that there is no chance of certificates expiring without our knowledge. Consequently, we need an active certificate management system. The Internet is well protected if everyone uses the Simple Socket Layer (SSL)/TLS protocols, but there are still exceptions to be found. In any event, as practically everything an organisation does touches the Internet somehow or other, it is essential to ensure that this methodology is maintained throughout its own networks with a well-conceived PKI, thus encrypting everything that passes both internally and externally. The risk is the loss of your organisation's intellectual property and associated assets, without which, its very presence is called into question. PKI is important and encryption lies at the heart of a PKI.

SUMMARY

In this section, we have looked at encryption in both its broadest terms and with respect to certificates and a PKI. The principles of encryption have been discussed, examples given and, in addition, a brief history of encryption has been covered. From this, the reader will have gained an understanding of how encryption works and how it is integrated into the concept of digital certificates and PKI. The widespread use of the Internet and cloud technologies has also been touched upon as this represents a primary application.

Chapter 6

Biometrics and public key infrastructure

The possibilities of biometric certificates

The author first started to think about biometrics and certificates in the early 1990s and, by the late 1990s, had formulated some ideas in this context and also incorporated some application design aids into the BANTAM Biometric and Token Technology Application Modelling Language. It would seem to make sense that, if identity verification was important, then biometrics might usefully be used alongside digital certificates. In its simplest form, this may have taken the shape of a biometric identity verification check being used to release a certificate, which might optionally contain the biometric. Bear in mind that in those days, biometrics were often in algorithmic form and therefore represented small amounts of code. For example, the leading hand geometry device created a biometric template which was just nine bytes in length. This could easily have been incorporated into all sorts of things, including, if required, a digital certificate.

In fact, the hand geometry device, together with a voice verification device, first sparked my attention towards biometrics, and I realised that, eventually, they would be used upon a large scale, but probably incorrectly. Most of the early devices created algorithmic biometric templates of a small size. There were numerous early fingerprint devices which were very efficient in this respect, plotting features upon an xy grid. And these were much more accurate than current devices which mostly work on grey scale pattern matching. Prof. John Daugman's early work on iris recognition created a relatively small iris code which was also highly accurate. For a while, things were going in the right direction until the great rush to implement biometrics for border control, when quality and accuracy were replaced by implementation convenience. However, that is another story entirely. Bear in mind also that, in the 1990s and early 2000s, several laptops started to appear with integral fingerprint readers, and there were all manner of initiatives which merged biometrics with smart cards (and still do). Many fingerprint reading devices worked by plotting features upon a fine grid, which was not unlike how police forensic departments traditionally worked. If a certain number of features matched, then the fingerprints were considered a match. The odd technique out was always face recognition which, in the early days, had all sorts of problems as the facial image is so easily changed or obscured.

DOI: 10.1201/9781003360674-6

In any event, early algorithmic-based biometric systems had the virtue of creating small-size templates which could be used on almost anything, from magnetic stripe cards to smart cards, or incorporated into other documents. In 1992, the author incorporated the code from a hand geometry template into the second (then unused) line of Optical Character Recognition (OCR) on a passport. I believe this was the first time that a biometric was *encoded* onto a passport. The first image of a biometric on a passport was undertaken by Argentinean Police Officer Juan Vucetich, who placed an image of his fingerprint on his own passport around 1900. So, the idea of using biometrics for border control was certainly not new. The merging of law enforcement and border control however was and had dramatic consequences. And, of course, the new 'smart' biometrics passport had provision for a public key infrastructure (PKI) which, initially, got into a real mess. Hopefully, this runs smoothly now.

Going back to the 1990s, there were many discussions around how these technologies might come together. The catalyst for such ideas was the smart card. The smart card could interact with computer devices and dedicated smart card readers and the chip on the card, while initially of limited capacity, was growing in size every day, while costs were continually coming down. Many laptop computers included smart card readers as standard fixtures. I still have one today which is working perfectly. Many point-of-sale terminals which once had magnetic stripe card readers were now going over to smart cards. Even bank automated teller machines (ATMs), which were notoriously slow at adopting new technologies, were systematically moving towards the use of smart cards. In fact, the term 'smart card' was something of a misnomer as there was very little intelligence within early examples. I always referred to them as 'chip cards' which was a more accurate description.

In any event, chip cards had tremendous potential which, even now, is hardly being realised. Some forward-thinking companies such as Precise Biometrics in Sweden experimented with 'match-on-card' technology in the early 2000s whereby they succeeded in placing a fingerprint reader on a device which wasn't exactly a chip card, but was not much thicker. Now, they have perfected the design to sit comfortably on a chip card. And so, not surprisingly, there was also talk of using chip cards with certificates. Certainly, certificates could be stored on chip cards and read from them by readers built into laptops or point-of-sale equipment. Indeed, this became a standard way of logging individuals onto networks in many high-security situations. Sometimes, the chip cards would simply contain a user ID and password, sometimes a certificate. If a biometric was used to first verify the identity of a user and then, upon verification, release a certificate, that would certainly be providing a high level of both user authentication and data encryption. Bear in mind that, as previously mentioned, most biometric techniques then were using proper algorithmic biometric matching and therefore tended to be more accurate (the alternative, as adopted for passports, is to simply compare images of biometrics using pattern matching, which is less reliable). A well-designed fingerprint biometric device could produce a small biometric template or code, which could be easily written to a chip card and which would provide a high degree of personal identity verification. The fingerprint reader could either be integral to the main device, such as a laptop, or simply configured as a serial/universal serial bus (USB) plug-in device. Siemens even marketed a very successful biometric mouse with a capacitive sensor where the third mouse button would be. Indeed, there were several such devices coming from the far east. In addition, there were several biometric products aimed at network security, some of them integrating with Microsoft's Active Directory, and others could, with a little effort, easily be incorporated into other corporate/ Lightweight Directory Access Protocol (LDAP) directories on UNIX or Linux. It is surprising that more government agencies and commercial entities did not adopt this idea, as it was a relatively simple one. This may have been through an inherent mistrust of biometrics, having been exposed to poor quality examples.

It seemed reasonable then to think about bringing biometrics and certificates together. There were two obvious ways in which this could be undertaken. The first was to use a biometric identity verification check to release a certificate and the second was to actually include a biometric template code into a certificate. This would, upon being presented as part of the handshake, require the user to authenticate using their biometric. It would still be possible to do this today, the issue was, and remains, one of standardisation. The technical fraternity would need to come up with a generic biometric template code which any device manufacturer could use. This would still allow for differentiation via the particular matching algorithm being used, but the personal data would be standardised. This would have been possible; however, trying to get several manufacturers to agree on a common format is always difficult. And then, trying to get such a format accepted as a standard could take years. No-one seemed to have the energy to do this back then. Today, with the concept of Open Source being far better established, it would no doubt be a little easier, but in the late 1990s, it was a step too far for most to contemplate. Both the biometrics and chip card communities were already having trouble sustaining themselves, and the concept of PKIs was also struggling to be accepted on a wider field.

With all technologies, adoption tends to follow a bell curve where, in the early years, proponents really struggle to get the idea across; then, everyone wants to use it until something new comes along and relegates it to a second-tier technique. It is the same in all industries. Some fundamentals endure, but many good ideas simply come and go. The three good ideas of PKI, chip cards and biometrics, were destined to never quite converge. However, that does not mean that they never will do so. There is always the possibility that someone will come up with a novel way of bringing them together.

Back in the 1990s, in order to help facilitate this, I included certificates and keys within the BANTAM Biometric and Token Technology Application Modelling Language which, in fact, was far more than just a modelling language and included a full procurement system with standardised templates for RFIs and RFPs as well as a supplier and project database. I later discovered that BANTAM was being actively used in various academic institutions for educational purposes. The core notation set remains freely available today.

Using BANTAM, it was possible to design an entire system, upon any scale, which utilised either a PKI or biometrics or chip cards or all three. In addition, it also catered for traditional system components such as databases, directories and networks as well as specific applications. It could also be used for process engineering and process re-engineering as well as having complete documentation for procurement, in a manner which was repeatable, scalable and which applied an appropriate rigour to the entire, end-to-end process. In fact, there is a book devoted to BANTAM which was published by Springer. It included a CD with many interesting templates and, of course, the initial symbol set. An updated notation set is available from the author.

Suffice it to say that it would have been perfectly feasible to integrate biometrics with both chip cards and the concept of a PKI. Adding a template field to the x.509 certificate specification would have been perfectly possible, if agreement could have been reached on its precise format. It then could have been utilised in a variety of ways and may have accelerated the initial usage of PKIs. As it is, PKIs have been a long time coming. Now, certificates and keys underpin almost everything in IT, but there is always room for innovation.

There is of course one underlying problem associated with the authentication part of PKI and that is the level of confidence you may have in the true identity of the person or device that is connecting to you. If you consider email for example. Assume that a certificate has been requested for Joe Soap and the email address of joe@soap.com. The certificate authority will check the email address to see if it exists and if it returns a message. If so, the certificate will be issued. And now, if you get the certificate and public key of Joe Soap at joe@soap.com, you will no doubt believe that you are connecting with Joe Soap. However, the truth is that you have no idea who you are connecting to. Fred Jones could have set up the email address of joe@soap.com. Or Susan Soap could have set up an alias of joe@soap.com. Or anyone else could have established that email address. The level of confidence you may have as to the true identity of who you are connecting to when using email certificates is actually quite low. With regard to machine addresses, a certificate may be issued for an i.p. address on a certain domain, but that is no guarantee of what that machine has on it or what it is set up to do, it may well have malware on it. However, it is with personal certificates that we really have limited confidence as to the true identity of the sender and, of course, no confidence at all when it comes to intent. Well, we can do nothing about intent, but we could increase the confidence as to the true identity of the user by using a biometric.

Even biometrics are limited as to the confidence one might have in the original registration authority. The rigour with which identities are checked prior to registering a biometric will vary enormously between countries and organisations. For example, the rigour with which passport applications are checked in some countries is very poor. Consequently, adding a biometric to the passport does not mean that the person concerned is who they claim to be. It does mean, however, that that person has registered their biometric against a claimed identity, and consequently, it may be verified in association with that claimed identity. You may rest assured that professional criminals will have several such passports, with different identities and the same biometric. The author proved how easy it is to do this many years ago.

So now, we have a biometric that is registered against a claimed identity and, wherever it is used, that claimed identity is verified (assuming that the live biometric matches the registered template). Now, if we tied that biometric to a digital certificate, for certain applications, we could require a remote identity verification via the biometric. We could achieve this by having the biometric template – a proper algorithmic code, embedded in the digital certificate. Now, when the handshake is undertaken, the person at the other end could be required to undertake a biometric identity verification using that particular code as the reference, and the result returned as a binary yes or no flag. Now, we would have a much higher confidence as to the identity of the person at the other end. But how could we do this given the size of a certificate and the sheer number of certificates in use? Well, one way would be to simply include a field within the certificate specification which set aside a certain number of bytes to be used for a biometric code or template. Most fingerprint biometric templates would fit into a compact code, as would iris recognition if undertaken properly. Similarly, hand geometry and others would be able to utilise this facility. From the perspective of the certificate, it would not really matter which biometric was used. If need be, the field could be preceded by a single letter to indicate the type of biometric being used, thus initiating an appropriate biometric reader.

The concept is raised, once again, in this book as it is an idea that is entirely feasible and which might be beneficial to high-security applications. It would address the authentication weakness of personal certificates. At present, anyone who has access to a laptop or other device which has a personal certificate on it can use that certificate to sign and encrypt messages. It does not mean that they are the person to whom the certificate was originally issued. The party at the other end, actually, has no idea who they are, only that they are using a particular certificate which, actually, may have been copied on to more than one device. A properly thought through biometric certificate would add another layer of security which could be invaluable for certain applications and which would solve this particular problem.

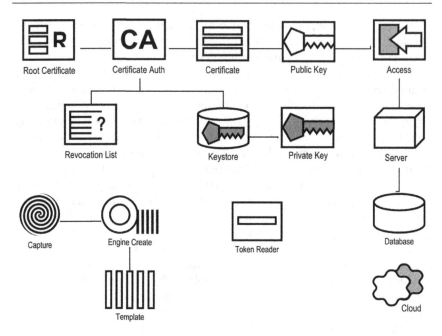

Figure 6.1 Some elements of the BANTAM notation.

It may be worth setting up a small government working group to explore the idea further. Certainly, it could be utilised in closed loop, official systems with little difficulty.

SUMMARY

In this section, biometrics in general have been discussed and a distinction made between algorithmic biometric templates and the pattern matching of images, which is not really a biometric at all as it is measuring an image rather than a physiological trait. It has been noted that the idea of biometric certificates was raised in the 1990s and that the author added certificate capabilities to the BANTAM symbol notation in order to incorporate a PKI into the design of other systems. An example of the notation has been provided in Figure 6.1. The concept of adding biometrics to certificates has been revisited and placed within a contemporary context.

Chapter 7

What is the conventional wider infrastructure?

Different infrastructure models explained

In 1994, Borland Delphi v.1 was released, and it caused something of a revolution in the field of application development. People had been discussing rapid application development and object-oriented programming at conferences and within development and academic circles, but we were not really practising what we preached. And then, along came Delphi. It was truly object oriented and including the practice of inheritance, making it easy for developers to create their own components. It had an IDE (Integrated Development Environment) which was way ahead of the competition and which was very intuitive in use. It produced code in units (we think that containers is a new idea, but Delphi started out on this road, and by v.3, you could actually deploy containers, Delphi called them packages, and re-use them among several applications). It used Object Pascal which is a very intuitive language producing human-readable code and is thus self-documenting. It had extremely good database connectivity and included two desktop databases, plus native connectivity to InterBase, one of the very best and most efficient databases ever built. It came with the ReportSmith reporting engine, a whole host of components and dialogues and much more. This was a developer's dream come true, and many middle bracket applications for commerce and industry were built with Delphi v.1. Why mention it here? Well, because it sat very comfortably with the manner in which programmers were developing applications, both within organisations, and those who were developing applications for market.

In those days, there were very clearly defined distinctions between the development function, the operations function and the project management function. If it was considered that another piece of organisational functionality would be desirable, the project management function would research the situation and come up with a design specification. The development function would build the necessary software, against this specification, and test it on the development platform. The operations function would test it again and, if all was well, it would be ported to the live environment. The organisation for whom I worked maintained twin, mirror-image data centres, separated geographically but connected by a high-bandwidth private network. Everything was backed up nightly, and everything worked. The

DOI: 10.1201/9781003360674-7

word 'outage' was not in our vocabulary because we didn't have any. We built the infrastructure ourselves, maintained around 3500 servers as well as a small number of mainframes and everything worked. Mostly because everything was designed and built in-house. We were also early advocates of Linux and Open Source (having used UNIX for years) and had many expert developers. And this was how many organisations worked, until people at senior management level started to interfere.

In 1996, Borland released Delphi v.2 which enlarged upon what they had already achieved but took the design to 32-bit level in order that developers could build applications for the new Windows 95 (which was never completely 32 bit). The client–server version of the development platform could truly develop enterprise wide systems for the Windows platform. The next year (1997) Delphi v.3 came along and included a great deal of Internet-related functionality and also offered the choice of compiling self-contained executables or building small units of code in 'packages' which, once deployed, could be utilised by multiple applications. Yes, in 1997, Borland already gave us containers that could be deployed anywhere on the network and referenced by multiple applications. But Delphi packages were robust units which were built within a rugged development environment which included the industry's best and fastest debugger and many helpful tools such as 'code insight' which checked code and almost wrote it for you, guaranteeing correct syntax. The superlative database connectivity remained and now included a new XML-based data component. There were also tools for SQL construction and checking, Database Desktop for constructing database tables in several different formats, a client-side version of InterBase and much more. In fact, Delphi v.3 was a better development platform than almost anything we have today. It was also properly documented with a variety of printed manuals. It remained truly object oriented and came with a stack of great components. It even had a separate CLX toolset for building Linux-compatible components. Indeed, several third-party development companies produced components for Delphi, including the wonderful TurboPower who produced excellent, well-documented, specialist components for a variety of tasks. This was 1997.

In industry, the trend among organisations who knew what they were doing was to use Linux servers and Windows on the desktop. This created some issues with Microsoft's Active Directory, but these could be readily solved from the Linux side. Still, people tended to maintain their own IT infrastructures and, therefore, remain in control of them. But inroads were being made into government, academia and industry by the giant software companies who were determined to become even bigger. And, frankly, their business ethics were practically zero. Which is how they succeeded, firstly in government circles and then further afield.

In 2001, we had Delphi v.6 which fully embraced the Internet and, in it's 'enterprise' form included ready built components for almost anything you could think of, including integration with Microsoft Office modules. All of the good things about Delphi were still there, but now there were many more of them. It really was the best development platform for Windows out there. In 2002, Delphi v.7 appeared and did it yet again but that was really the last of the proper Borland releases. There was a Delphi v.8 which was simply Delphi for the.net environment but, after that, it was passed on to Embarcadero who continue with it today.

The year 2001 was a pivotal year for many reasons, especially politically. But 2001/2002 was also pivotal for many organisations who had started to outsource functionality or bring in to the organisation monolithic applications from unscrupulous suppliers which they would never be able to support themselves. The Internet was changing everything and organisations became increasingly dependent upon the Internet when, in truth, they did not need to. Following the outsourcing of major functions came the outsourcing of personnel and the loss of the specialist skills which had built their good quality infrastructures to start with. And different industry buzzwords started to appear which served only to obscure and de-skill even further. 'Agile' was one of these words which changed well-proven development and test cycles into chaotic situations where nobody seemed accountable for anything anymore. Other phrases such as 'buy don't build' were heavily promoted, especially by those with a vested interest in doing so. But everything you bought seemed incompatible with what you had, so you bought more in order to fill the gaps and so on. Meanwhile, organisations in all sectors continued to lose experienced staff and relied instead on less experienced staff developing applications for the Internet, which were less robust. The word 'outages' would start to appear now. By about 2012, it was all very different and, throughout the next decade, there would be a massive emphasis on the cloud, especially by the four largest organisations who, between them, own most of it.

It is hard to believe that almost all government agencies, academia and most of the commercial world have all fallen for this and have, effectively, lost control of their IT while paying at least twice as much for it. On top of all of this, they pay exorbitant amounts to management consultants who just tell them to put everything in the cloud. Having been stupid enough to do so, they are hit again, this time by technology providers who insist upon changing all the development methodologies, using phrases such as 'rapid development', although it were an absolute necessity. In parallel, solid, proven development languages have given way to script-based languages – lots of them. So, any one service or application might have code in four or five different languages. Maintained by whom? Very often by outsourced IT service providers.

We have gone from a world of IT infrastructures which made sense to one which makes no sense at all. Furthermore, organisations in all sectors have paid through the nose to place themselves in such a position. And they have, in many cases, completely lost control of their IT in the process, including all of their critical data. And they have, in parallel, suffered from massive skills erosion.

The old world operated in-house physical IT infrastructures which were easily maintained by skilled personnel who understood them intimately, mostly because they had built them in the first place. If they needed to be expanded upon, this could easily be planned and executed, while maintaining a suitable technical and security rigour. Applications were built as and when needed. There was no paranoia over 'rapid' development. It didn't need to be rapid, it needed to be good. And it was. Programmes didn't fall over and, if any issues were discovered after an application had moved to the live environment, they were focused on immediately and fixed, but such occurrences were rare. Hardware was inexpensive, server motherboard 'cards' could be bought and installed in 19″ racks, with everything clearly labelled and all i.p. addresses clearly indicated. Implementing a public key infrastructure (PKI) manually was straightforward enough. Security received an equal focus with a very strong rigour applied throughout and maintained by a separate team. The only externally facing servers were web servers which were in their own zone, behind firewalls and load balancers, all of which were understood and configured by in-house staff who had the knowledge to do so. Major IT projects were undertaken with ease because they were properly planned by skilled personnel. At that time, within the organisation for whom I worked, nothing phased us. We took everything in our stride and built what we needed as we went. It was a good model because we could also support everything properly (as it was us who built it in the first place). If we needed more servers, we bought the hardware, built an operating system image for it, attached it to storage and that was it. No one said that the process took too long because they knew that it was undertaken properly.

But those times have sadly gone. Nowadays, many organisations have systematically moved core IT functionality into the cloud. They have placed their operational data and intellectual assets into someone else's hands, without giving a thought to who that someone really is. People tend to think of the cloud as if it really is somewhere in the sky. They forget that absolutely everything that is in the cloud is on somebody's servers somewhere. Or, more to the point, on somebody's servers and disc arrays. This is physical infrastructure, maintained by the big companies previously referred to, in various parts of the world. These companies might claim that they are hosting the cloud on UK or US servers, but that means nothing. They might even have a token data centre which they could show you. That also means nothing. The reality is that the bulk of their servers and disc arrays will be deployed anywhere in the world where it is inexpensive to do so. This could be in Indonesia, Mexico, India, anywhere. And that is where your organisation's critical data will be held. Someone has to maintain that physical infrastructure. Again, the least expensive option will be chosen, and you will have no idea whatsoever who these people are and what access they have to your data. If they have access to the physical infrastructure, they have access to any of the data which reside upon it.

If all that isn't worrying enough, we now have new development methodologies whereupon perfectly adequate applications are being trashed as people instead develop everything again as 'microservices' which may be thought of almost as Delphi 'units'. And these microservices run in containers, which may be thought of as Delphi 'packages'. The trouble is, these containers are volatile and may be created and destroyed at will or moved around upon the physical infrastructure in order to attempt load balancing. This plays havoc with PKI which really wants to know where everything is all the time. The increase in processing that this entails is enormous and what is promoted as 'rapid' is, in truth, anything but. Furthermore, as I have discovered while researching this book, even the providers of these new technologies don't really understand them.

The ancient Egyptians understood the distinction between order and chaos. In an ordered world, things worked and useful progress was made. In a chaotic world, things broke and everything stalled or went backwards. They were always conscious of this dichotomy and, consequently, placed a great emphasis on proper training and doing things properly in a tried and tested manner. Interestingly, they prophesied, in the Middle Kingdom, that the 'end of days' would be preceded by chaos. Well, we certainly have a chaotic approach to IT and IT development at the moment. In the new world, we need PKIs more than ever, but they are not so easy to implement on cloud-based infrastructures in which things move around. This will be covered in more depth in the next chapter.

SUMMARY

This chapter has served to make the distinction between traditional ways of building and running an IT infrastructure and more modern ways of doing the same. The cloud has been introduced and points made around the physical infrastructure which underpins it. It has been stressed that the invisibility of your applications and data within the cloud is not a good thing. Neither is the disruption caused by building everything again and then paying for it, year on year, while losing trained personnel in the process. The tried and tested ways of going about development and managing a PKI have been, in many cases, replaced with a chaotic scramble to adopt new technologies at any cost. This is not a good thing.

Chapter 8

Kubernetes, containers and PKI

The container model and its implications for PKI

It all starts with the concept of microservices, small sections of code which are meant to perform one simple task and nothing else. The evangelists behind this movement will claim that this means that each microservice, being a small block of code to perform a single function, will necessarily be more robust than a larger block of code which performs several related functions or, indeed, a complete application. This of course is complete nonsense and implies that modern developers are simply not capable of writing complex code or writing code which is properly debugged and tested before being moved to the live environment. Furthermore, it removes accountability from the larger application and dramatically increases the processing power needed to run the entire application. The word 'application' has been largely replaced with the word 'stack' to indicate the vast number of microservices being run in order to provide even a basic service. This may easily run into thousands. If we embrace the idea that a single developer responsible for a microservice will necessarily write better code, because the microservice is small and only performs a single function, this breaks down when one considers that the same developer will probably be responsible for a dozen or so microservices (or possibly many more) and so will become increasingly confused by the bigger picture and, therefore, by the code written for each microservice. Furthermore, it is, for the developer, a frustrating manner in which to write code as they rarely see the fruits of their labour, just snapshots of small chunks of the overall 'stack'.

I watched a presentation from the IT head of a large, well-known organisation which had a perfectly well-functioning IT model. She proudly claimed that the move to microservices only took around seven or eight months and that, while their IT costs virtually doubled within this period, one must expect to pay for such things. Of course, their IT costs never did come back down to where they were because they were now paying out more to third-party companies for support. She also proudly claimed that they were now using other people's infrastructure (the cloud) as they could then obviate themselves from any support issues, even though they were paying even more for this. Then, she very proudly claimed that the success of moving to microservices was obvious because, previously, they had only 143 application services to maintain and that now they had in excess of 2200. In fact, she had increased the risk to the operation as a whole by a factor of slightly more than 15. She had increased the complexity of the operation to the point that it was almost unsupportable, she had destroyed any coding rigour that might have previously endured and she had significantly increased the cost of IT to the organisation concerned, not just in the immediate term but perpetually. This lady (and there are increasingly more female IT directors) will no doubt get a bonus for her good work and then leave for a higher paid position elsewhere. Meanwhile, she has saddled the organisation with substantially more cost, in order to do the same thing that they were already doing, but with different technologies. Her last slide was a picture of the 'stack' which was unintelligible, even on the big screen, because it was at such a fine scale, in turn, because it was so complex. And that, apparently was only a part of it. Within any organisation, it is important to be able to map out your entire IT operation, including all the links, the i.p. addresses and where it touches the outside world. If you cannot do this, then you cannot possibly support the organisational IT model. But then, individuals such as the lady I mentioned don't care about this because they spend the organisation's money by outsourcing support for almost everything. This is a one way street, the truth of which many have found to their cost and embarrassment. It also, inevitably, leads to failure because those to whom support is outsourced do not understand the entire operational model of the organisation concerned. Consequently, when something crashes, and it will, they do not understand the knock-on implications. And then, you have 'outages' while yet more consultants are brought in to try and sort out the mess. Yes, that's right, the whole thing is ridiculous but it is happening increasingly with government agencies and commercial enterprises alike.

From a coding perspective, microservices are what we used to call a code block. A block of code within a unit which contained several such blocks. The benefit of having them together in one unit, whether it was a complete application, a DLL (dynamically linked library) or a Delphi package, was that they could be built, debugged and tested together. Consequently, the developer would have confidence that the entire application or package worked well as a holistic entity. Furthermore, it could be maintained as such. It might be a particular application, let's say a personnel application, that stood alone and functioned in its own right, but which also linked to other applications, such as payroll and took dynamic updates from it as required. Thus, the application model for the entire organisation could easily be mapped, together with all the connections both internal and external. The organisation that I worked for had a large, active panel situated within the primary support team, which had every single server on it and how it connected to everything else. In addition, that layer could be drilled down further to show what was running on every server. If anything stopped, it would light up in red and was immediately addressed. It's hard to imagine how they could have done this with microservices.

Nevertheless, organisations will move to microservices because IT directors and senior managers (who have been influenced by suppliers) will convince the non-technical that they are a good idea. They will place themselves on a pathway to spiralling costs, IT outages and the loss of control over their own data. Whether the reader thinks that they are a good idea or otherwise might depend upon their experience within the broader IT world. The proposal for microservices will be speed of delivery. It will be possible to develop and deploy faster than it was previously. Yes, but no-one asks whether it is actually important to be able to develop and deploy faster than it was before, and in any event, we are only speaking of the deployment of small blocks of code. Having a faster turnaround of applications and functions is not necessarily better. There is an equal argument for operational stability, with any changes carefully considered, developed and tested properly, and then, finally, deployed into the live environment. But another buzz word has come along to support the idea of microservices and fast deployment and that is 'DevOps'. Under the banner of DevOps, the technology evangelists claim that it is ridiculous to have separate teams for development, project management and operations as this represents 'silo' thinking. Instead, they should all be mixed together under one leadership model in order that developers can use the new technologies to develop whatever they like, quickly, and deploy it to the live environment with virtually no testing, other than what is automated by their tools. In addition, they have introduced new working titles such as 'cloud architects', 'infrastructure coders', 'DevOps engineers' and 'operations engineers', thus creating their own silos, but without being based upon a solid understanding. This revolutionary thinking is what has, in many organisations, destroyed what was a reliable IT model and replaced it with a chaotic, anything goes, mentality. Is it any wonder that so many things are breaking? Everywhere you go, services are being denied because of 'IT problems' some of which continue for days and weeks. These are IT problems which we did not previously have, so what is going wrong? Well, the concept of DevOps for one and, within this model, the associated concept of microservices. It could work for you, but be careful. Mostly, it adds complexity and support issues. I have raised important issues about this new application development methodology because it is important that organisations fully understand the implications of working this way. Adding complication and losing control are among the more serious of these implications. In the case of containers, once established as a working methodology, these tend to multiply exponentially. What starts off as dozens can quickly become hundreds and hundreds can quickly become thousands or even hundreds of thousands. Managing this environment manually quickly becomes impossible, and so, additional layers are added in the form of service meshes and more. With respect to public key infrastructures (PKIs) and certificates, an organisation may quickly find that it is having to manage thousands or even hundreds of thousands of certificates. Undertaking this task manually is out of the question, and so, automation is brought in. Now the task is, hopefully, accomplished, but you have lost control of it completely. Furthermore, if buying certificates from a certificate authority (CA), the associated costs will also rise exponentially. All of this additional complexity and additional cost is leading right back to where you started. Your applications still perform the same tasks for you. You still have the same organisational requirements. But you have dramatically increased the complexity and cost of your IT operation. Even more serious is that you have lost control of it. It now resides upon someone else's infrastructure, for which you are paying an additional cost, and, via automation layers, you no longer know what is really going on. With respect to certificates and PKI, your costs will undoubtedly rise significantly and it is likely that you will need to engage yet another third party in order to manage it all. All of this is in support of the idea of rapid application development and deployment using DevOps. However, do you actually need to do this? In any case, it is a myth as the additional complexity will slow things down considerably. These factors need to be taken into consideration.

So, let us get back to where it all started with the concept of microservices. Now, the thing with microservices is that you have to host them somewhere. Where do you put them? The answer is that you host them within containers (remember 1997 and Delphi packages?). And where do you put the containers? Ah! A good question. They need to, ultimately, sit on a conventional server based infrastructure but where? The evangelists will tell you that they have to be placed in the cloud. And then, they can be started up and shut down at will, but why would you want to do this? Also, they can be moved around automatically in the interests of load balancing. Load balancing? Whose load balancing? Certainly not yours, because you no longer own the infrastructure. What they (the cloud suppliers) are really saying is that they will move *your* containers around in order to facilitate load balancing on *their* servers. The problem is, if your container is moved to a different server with a different i.p. address, services which access this container and its certificates will need to know where to look for it. This will involve an active service layer to maintain control over all of these connections. This entails further complexity, processing power and cost. Nevertheless, the idea of containers sitting on top of an operating system, but only containing those elements of the operating system that they actually need, is an attractive one to some. It does of course also entail an enormous amount of duplication. The usually provided schematic layout of this idea is something as shown in Figure 8.1.

In this theoretical model, there is a single host operating system (but bear in mind that this has to be hosted on a hardware server) and running on top of this is a runtime engine which is responsible for running and managing your containers, an additional processing layer which will consume resources. And then, presumably sitting on the same server are your containers. Now,

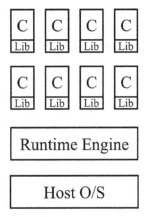

Figure 8.1 Theoretical container model.

each one of these containers will host either a complete application, or a service, or maybe simply a function (similar to a DLL). However, this application, service or function cannot run without access to the functionality inherent within the operating system. Consequently, each container must also have any runtime environments, libraries and other components that it needs from the operating system in order to run, and this requirement might be substantial. If you have just eight containers, then this is duplicated, more or less, eight times (each container might require a slightly different set of O/S resources). However, if you have 800 containers, which is entirely feasible, then the resources are duplicated 800 times and require 800 times the processing power.

In addition, each service running in a container will require its own certificates. So, under a conventional model, a server would have had a handful of certificates for authentication and encryption purposes. Now, if there are 800 containers associated with this particular server, it has 800 sets of certificates, plus the original certificates for the server itself. Furthermore, these containers might be taken down and new ones might appear, fairly frequently. Each time this happens, it impacts the certificate inventory. The effect that the container model has on an organisational PKI is enormous. The complexity of managing all of these certificates, some of which might be self-signed, others purchased from a third-party CA, is beyond what may easily be managed manually. For most, it will require the acquisition of an automated certificate management system. This will in itself add considerable cost as well as, initially, impacting the smooth running of the IT function. Furthermore, it represents a one way street as, having gone down this road, and lost the ability to manage your own certificates, there is no turning back, at least not while you are running a microservice and container model under a DevOps strategy. The organisational PKI, within such a scenario, will grow to dangerously unmanageable proportions, except under automation.

In fact, the container model overall has exactly this problem. As the number of containers grow, almost exponentially, the ability to manage them declines. And so, other layers must be added to the already complex model (Figure 8.2).

In the diagram below, we have added the other essential components of the cloud-based container management services, which all container clusters require, plus application services, such as the PKI management layer, plus the inevitable service mesh in order to keep the whole thing going. The service mesh manages and controls all the communications and network traffic between the containers. It enables services to discover each other and undertakes intelligent routing in order to keep the messages flowing as they should, including from the various application programming interfaces (APIs). When the number of containers grows to thousands, this network of traffic calls back and forth can become extremely complicated, to the degree that they become impractical to manage manually. Like certificates, they require some sort of automated management. This is where the service mesh comes in. It works using network proxies which are attached to each container (more complexity). This is popularly known as the Sidecar pattern. Using these proxies, the service mesh builds its own knowledge of the greater system of containers and allows for communication between them. It also allows for the application of policies and rules for all the connections and includes components for telemetry so that, in theory at least, a view of the overall system may be created, and it includes a component for creating and applying certificates. The PKI management system has to be aware of these

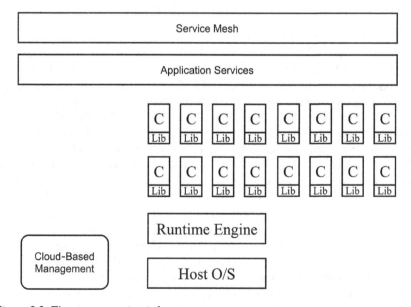

Figure 8.2 The ever growing infrastructure.

other layers and work with them effectively. For example, who is going to supply the certificates? The service mesh might supply self-signed certificates for securing traffic between containers, but some containers may be required to make external connections, in which case they will require certificates from a trusted CA. The PKI management system should really take overall control. It might decide to use the certificate creation capabilities of the service mesh, in tandem with its own calls out to CAs. If all of this sounds complicated, it is becoming even more complicated with more layers being added as we go. One of these new layers aspires to server-less applications with a simplified build and deploy method which stays within the container group. But does that not cut across some of these other technologies? Yes, it does. But, at the same time, it relies upon them, especially the service mesh, in order to provide its own capabilities. If such a layer has been deployed within the organisational IT model, then the PKI management layer needs to know about it.

One of the often quoted advantages of these new technology layers is the speed with which microservices and applications might be built and deployed. But this very capability is a big problem for a PKI. It may mean that thousands or tens of thousands of certificates are continually being created, used for a short time and destroyed. The amount of additional processing and network traffic will be considerable. There will also be a concurrent rise in cost for the organisation concerned. The continually repeated mantra of fast development becomes meaningless if there is an exponential rise in complexity and cost. Complexity also increases risk, which means extra attention must be paid to security. That also equates to increased cost. It can all be done and most of it may be automated, but we must also understand the increased cost in real terms which, for most organisations, will be very considerable. In any event, for an organisation that has embraced the DevOps concept, together with containers, code repositories, service meshes and more, it will be essential to deploy some sort of automated PKI management system. The certificate creation capabilities within a service mesh (which may also be undertaken manually in code) may be sufficient for many containers, but any which are outward facing or otherwise call third parties will still require certificates issued by a trusted CA. But both types must be managed. This could be undertaken manually with calls from certain containers made directly to CAs by code written by the developers. However, with many developers coding within a given organisation, this could quickly get out of hand. Certificate renewal in particular could become a problem, and there might be an unnecessary expense in certificates which are hardly used. There needs to be some intelligence applied here, and some rationalisation of the certificate estate and how it is used. The most popular containers are called Kubernetes, and there has been much thought put into them as a development model, but rather less with respect to a PKI. In addition, many other components and services have been written to interact with Kubernetes. One of the popular service meshes is Istio and, again, much thought has been put into this as a mechanism, including self-signed certificate creation, but who is managing this? There are also code repositories and many other blocks of new technology in support of the DevOps idea. Also, there is a good deal of documentation, although some of it is quite complex and will be beyond the typical Senior Manager or Director. Existing developers will be comfortable with the script-like languages such as YAML but will still need to learn many new tricks and embrace new concepts. For them, all this might be interesting, but is it necessary? We have the 'how'. What we don't have is the 'why?' For PKIs, the DevOps fashion is a disaster in one way, in that it seriously over complicates what was already a complicated model. In another sense, it creates a huge opportunity for PKI vendors to also embrace this model and come up with more automated services of their own. For the end user organisation, it means considerably more cost and complexity in order to do what you were already doing. You might be able to do it a little more quickly now (although this is debatable) but first, you will go through a huge learning curve, accompanied by an equally huge and ongoing expense. However, the most important factor for many will be the loss of control if you put everything in the cloud and then automate it. If you decide to embrace DevOps, then you need to look closely at Kubernetes (or their equivalents) and what this means for your own PKI. If you are already working with a PKI vendor, then you may like to discuss this with them. You will probably find that they are already struggling with the idea and will offer you a completely automated service which you have no sight of. Behind the scenes, they will then attempt to plug into the various layers of technology that now make up your IT model or 'stack'. They will undoubtedly get something working, but what? And will they have spotted any operational or security-related weaknesses? Of course not, because they do not really understand your organisation in depth.

SUMMARY

In this chapter, the broader container model has been discussed and the reader introduced to the concept of service meshes, server-less development and other ideas. Most importantly, the impact which all of these technologies has upon an organisational PKI has been stressed. The primary point being the exponential rise in complexity as thousands or tens of thousands of certificates replace what had been perhaps a few tens of certificates. This requires considerably more management. There will also be a lot more PKI-related processing and, of course, cost. The introduction of new technologies typically spells additional cost in order to do the same thing. In this case, the additional cost could be significant and organisations should take this into consideration when considering whether or not to go down this road.

Chapter 9

Trust and certificates

The original concept has changed

Within the original public key infrastructure (PKI) concept, there was quite a heavy emphasis upon trust. Between registration authorities and certificate authorities (CAs), actions were performed which tested the trust that was to be associated with a newly created and issued certificate. CAs really would make background checks upon a company wishing to buy one or more digital certificates. They would check that a company or organisation was properly listed, who its executive officers were, whether it had ever been involved in any untoward activities and so on. Lastly, it would contact the company at the address given in order to satisfy itself that the company or organisation really did exist and that it was what it claimed to be. This level of trust associated with the issuance of a digital certificate was very important indeed. Furthermore, a CA would pride itself on the efforts that it would make in order to substantiate the bona fides of a given organisation. After all, there were not that many organisations using certificates, and the CAs were eager to differentiate themselves in order to attract business. These were the good old days of early PKI when almost nobody had heard of the concept outside of a few who were interested in encryption, and even among this group, it was often thought that a PKI was unnecessarily complex. After all, encryption had been around for a long time and there were plenty of viable ways of using it, without creating a full PKI. Furthermore, these people had an entirely different concept of trust.

Slowly, very slowly, the idea of using a PKI took root and was accelerated greatly by the Internet and the use of the https protocol with Transport Layer Security (TLS). Now, it was necessary for any reputable organisation with a web site to use the https protocol and this meant using certificates issued by a trusted provider, i.e., a CA. But now, there were plenty of people wanting certificates, and CAs had merely to exist in order to do good business. The once careful and comprehensive checks that they would have made against an organisation requesting a certificate had now been reduced to simply checking that the web site domain really existed and was accessible. If that was the case, the organisation in question could buy any number of certificates from the CA. The CA now had no idea of who was really behind the web site. After all, anyone can build a web site and get it hosted

DOI: 10.1201/9781003360674-9

by an Internet service provider (ISP) who will also be only too pleased to oblige, for a suitable fee. A web site could present a purely fictitious organisation, describing a host of activities which they do not actually perform, with photographs of board members taken from readily available stock images. Such a site will have no problem at all buying certificates to associate with its domain name. Such a site could also have a 'private' area which hosted the exchange of all manner of dubious information and other activities, but it will still have no trouble presenting itself as trusted.

And so, the concept of trust, as associated with a digital certificate is now entirely different from what was originally intended. When such a certificate is used, all we really know is that the certificate is being used. We have absolutely no idea who is really using it. This was pointed out within Chapter 6 when discussing biometrics. Similarly, we have no idea whether the organisation, as presented on the web site, does in fact exist, or whether it is, actually, quite a different organisation altogether. The use of digital certificates is certainly helpful when used to encrypt communications in association with a suitable algorithm, but the trust model is perhaps not as strong as we have been lead to believe. Even CAs may not be as trustworthy as we assume and, certainly, their role in validating the bona fides of organisations who have been issued with certificates is not what it used to be. It is currently possible to buy certificates from any of the popular providers with a minimal amount of data exchange. If you have a web site and a valid email address, you should have no problem obtaining digital certificates. That, of course, does not mean that either you or the organisation that you are representing is trustworthy.

The distinction between self-signed certificates and those bought from a CA has already been made. And yet, the number of self-signed certificates in use would probably dwarf that of commercially provided examples. That is not necessarily a problem if they are being used on and between servers within an organisational infrastructure, primarily for encryption purposes. However, they still need to be properly constructed, annotated and managed. If this is not the case, then trust will be affected in another sense, especially with regard to expiration dates which may have been set unrealistically long to start with and then forgotten about altogether. Or the people who originally created them may have left the organisation and there may be a number of certificates in circulation that no one is actually aware of. This may be due to poor in-place policies with respect to certificates and the organisational PKI.

If certificates are created by your own CA, perhaps within a service mesh or otherwise sitting on the edge of your cluster of containers, they are effectively self-signed and created and destroyed at will. There may be a very large number of these due to the large number of connections between containers passing data. This is very useful from the encryption perspective as we don't want any data breaches (assuming someone has successfully hacked into your cluster of containers, which should not happen). However, the only trust element is that the certificates appear to come from your own CA. However, as almost anyone could create a certificate, then a certificate which looks like it was created by your own CA when, in fact, it was not, may appear in the /etc/kubernetes/pki directory and might be actively used. Furthermore, in addition to the root CA, it is possible to create intermediate CAs to issue certificates for specific purposes. A typical file path structure for the keys and certificates might end up looking like this;

```
/etc/kubernetes/pki/etcd/ca.key
/etc/kubernetes/pki/etcd/ca.crt
/etc/kubernetes/pki/apiserver-etcd-client.key
/etc/kubernetes/pki/apiserver-etcd-client.crt
/etc/kubernetes/pki/ca.key
/etc/kubernetes/pki/ca.crt
/etc/kubernetes/pki/apiserver.key
/etc/kubernetes/pki/apiserver.crt
/etc/kubernetes/pki/apiserver-kubelet-client.key
/etc/kubernetes/pki/apiserver-kubelet-client.crt
/etc/kubernetes/pki/front-proxy-ca.key
/etc/kubernetes/pki/front-proxy-ca.crt
/etc/kubernetes/pki/front-proxy-client.key
/etc/kubernetes/pki/front-proxy-client.crt
/etc/kubernetes/pki/etcd/server.key
/etc/kubernetes/pki/etcd/server.crt
/etc/kubernetes/pki/etcd/peer.key
/etc/kubernetes/pki/etcd/peer.crt
/etc/kubernetes/pki/etcd/healthcheck-client.key
/etc/kubernetes/pki/etcd/healthcheck-client.crt
/etc/kubernetes/pki/sa.key
/etc/kubernetes/pki/sa.pub
```

The code necessary to create a CA is quite straightforward, using command line tools such as easyrsa or openssl. In other words, it is just as easy to create CAs and certificates for a container cluster in the cloud as it ever was to create a certificate for a single server on your own infrastructure. In both cases, the certificates may usefully be used in order to encrypt data, but who actually has control over the certificates? From a trust perspective, this does not represent a particularly strong position, especially if you now have a much greater number of coders producing things for your container cluster. Furthermore, these coders may or may not be your own staff. Increasingly, there is a tendency for organisations to reduce their own salaried head count and outsource functions such as IT. This means that you may have a team of coders, probably from another country, who you know absolutely nothing about. One of their managers will have signed a statement of terms and conditions with your organisation, but this means nothing. You don't know who, among such a team, has the necessary authority to create a CA, anywhere, and then issue certificates from it, which you also know absolutely nothing about. This may all work fine. However, if someone with malicious intent managed to infiltrate this team, they could set things up in a way which could be harmful to your organisation. This is always the case when you outsource critical functions such as IT, but it can get very messy if you have also embraced the DevOps philosophy.

So how should you go about it. Well, firstly, if you haven't already done so, don't outsource the IT function. Secondly, and this was highlighted earlier in this work, it should be possible, even with containers, to create a complete plan of your entire IT estate. If using clusters of containers, this could be done at a high level, and then further plans showing the detail of each cluster and how it communicates, both internally and externally. When you have this detailed and accurate view, you can see where it is advantageous to use certificates and for what purpose. Understanding purpose is important. You may or may not want to have certificates for every single container. When you have this detailed map of the IT estate, both in and out of the cloud, you may then build your PKI accordingly. This may be undertaken manually, or you might do so in conjunction with a PKI management system which can search for certificates and bring them under a single point of control. There also needs to be a very strict rigour with respect to the creation of new certificates, what they are used for and what the expiry dates will be. Naturally, this entails segregation of duties with key members of staff responsible for the PKI overall. At least then, you would have a certain level of trust in place. If third-party developers are allowed to spin up CAs and issue certificates however and whenever they like, things will start to get very messy indeed from a PKI point of view. Even if you have a monolithic PKI system which might discover these certificates and register them for a while, there would still be very little trust involved. If certain containers require third-party certificates from an established CA, then who makes these decisions? And based on what? If absolutely anyone within the development team is allowed to specify this, then your costs will likely escalate fairly substantially.

There is already a trust issue inherent within the PKI model, as has been previously identified. It is important to ensure that this does not become magnified under a DevOps strategy which brings in containers and service meshes. These days, more than ever, it makes sense to have a small, dedicated PKI team who can oversee all of this and ensure that everything is attended to according to an appropriate rigour. It would be a mistake to leave this in the hands of an army of coders, whether they be internal or external to the organisation. The same applies if you use a specialist PKI management system. You need properly trained individuals who understand exactly what is happening within your IT environment, as well as the management system itself. They may then hold responsibility for your certificate estate.

Getting back to trust with respect to third-party CAs, they can check things like domain names and email addresses but their main purpose in life is to sell certificates. They know little about who they are really selling them to. This reality needs to be taken into consideration within your greater IT security model. It also needs to be borne in mind when designing your cloud-based environment. Where business-related transactions are involved, remember what being presented with a digital certificate *really* means and ensure that there is a security-related rigour that runs like a seam throughout your operational policies and procedures.

SUMMARY

In this chapter, the thorny question of trust has been considered from various perspectives. The situations which could cause your certificate inventory to grow exponentially have also been considered as well as the methodologies for creating certificates for use within your cluster of containers. The changing role of trusted CAs has additionally been noted. Within a PKI, it is easy to make all manner of assumptions, but we should tread carefully, especially if embracing a DevOps model, in which case it would be wise to assign a small, dedicated team to manage the organisational PKI, as well as becoming a reference and centre of excellence for others within the organisation to use.

Chapter 10

How may a localised infrastructure work?

Keeping things simple

We have been considering the brave new world of cloud-based container systems and all that they entail, especially the additional complexity which they bring to public key infrastructure (PKI). However, it remains very easy for organisations to build and maintain their own IT infrastructures, without going anywhere near the cloud. In addition, the experience of doing so will place them in a very strong position with regard to the ongoing support and maintenance of the various systems involved. It would also provide the invaluable opportunity to document everything fully, and this is something which rarely happens when things are outsourced or moved into the cloud and hardly ever happens within a DevOps environment. If all three of these factors are combined, which is increasingly the case, then it might be useful to ask for a full set of documentation, including system diagrams and code, and see what is presented.

When affordable and dependable computers first arrived, they were something of a novelty and were quickly put to use for office-based tasks. It is no surprise that some of the very first applications were word processors and spreadsheets, followed by compact desktop databases. A large organisation may, at this time, have been hosting a mainframe computer upon which critical data was stored and which may have been used for preparing information for accounting purposes or to manage a complicated function for the organisation involved (for example, reservation systems for airlines). With the advent of personal computers, it was quickly realised that these devices could easily be networked together and information thus shared easily between departments. Specialised network cards and network management software such as Novell NetWare (which was compact and powerful) appeared and, with the addition of a simple hub (a small piece of hardware featuring an array of network ports), a network could be up and running in no time. When organisations who had gone down this route wanted to use powerful software across all the computers within the network, this was achieved via a client/server model in which the main software was installed upon one computer designated as the 'server' while all the other computers had a lightweight version of the programme (the 'client' application) installed and this communicated with the host on the server.

And so, computers started to be differentiated between those designed for desktop use and those designed to be servers. The latter started to be built to a better specification, with better power supplies, sometimes the ability to use more than one processor and often the ability to use more memory. They had basic graphics capabilities and were often administered via a command line, sometimes on a 'green screen' attached visual display device. Applications such as databases were perfect for the client–server model and many started to appear, including the excellent InterBase, which was lightweight, fast and scalable. Organisations could easily build applications for themselves and most did so. This was an advantage as they held all the code and could easily extend or modify their own applications as required by the operation and, the truth was that, in many cases, the basic applications for databases, spreadsheets and word processors actually met all the requirements of a great many organisations. There was simply no need for the bloated, monolithic applications which we see everywhere today. For most organisations, this probably remains the case.

If you had a large group of servers within a typical computer room and running 24 hours a day, as they mostly would be, they tended to generate heat. And so, special computer rooms were built in which a stable environment could be maintained via air conditioning, even if the rest of the building didn't have it. These were also made physically secure in order that only those qualified to do so had access. This is how data centres evolved. Telephone lines could be used to extend the organisational reach between buildings, cities and even countries. From a local perspective, private lines could be used between data centres and offices for security reasons. Using off the shelf desktop computers and servers, it was easy to build and maintain an organisational network with relatively little effort and relatively little expense, especially if you understood what you really needed and why.

As time went on, things would become properly organised with defined duties allocated to the IT 'staff' who would themselves develop specialist skills. Their primary function was to keep everything running while administration staff could use the computers and services which they provided. This was an excellent state of affairs. Organisations had a slight increase in personnel costs but this was more than offset by the additional functionality and associated efficiencies which they enjoyed. Many would hold that this was how it should have stayed. Security was not much of an issue as the only traffic leaving the network were email messages and these went through a gateway via the email server and on to a third-party external network (provided by the telephone companies).

Networks such as that described could be built and maintained by practically anyone. The main operating systems available were firstly different versions of DOS, such as Microsoft DOS, DR DOS (which was excellent) and others, plus early UNIX-like systems. With the advent of Microsoft Windows and other graphical user interfaces, things really took off on the desktop and organisations were building great applications for themselves in languages such as C and C++. When Delphi first appeared, this revolutionised things from the application development perspective (there was also Visual Basic from Microsoft but it was not really comparable). In academia, UNIX was preferred for most things.

Hardware was advancing quickly with improved, faster processors, cheaper memory and better facilities built into motherboards. However, you still needed power supplies, cases, disc drives and hard discs, but why duplicate these things for every single server? In response to this question, simplified server 'cards' were developed which separated out the processing and network connectivity from data storage. These cards could be slotted into a frame within a 19″ rack which, in turn, could host a large number of servers with just one (or preferably two – one for backup) power supply and cooling system. Data storage was achieved by arrays of high specification hard discs as network-attached storage (NAS) clusters which would be duplicated and backed up automatically every night. Thus, the data centre could remain as one large, air conditioned room; furthermore, with uninterruptable power supplies installed, confidence in reliable operation no matter what occurred was high. Whether this 'data centre' was simply a locked room within the main office building (as was commonplace), or a proper, secured data centre in its own purpose-built building, it was actually a very straightforward proposition when it came to maintenance. For additional security, the data centre would be duplicated with identical facilities in two geographically separated locations, ensuring a degree of disaster recovery if something went badly wrong at one location. Still, the cost was manageable and the maintenance straightforward by properly trained staff who worked for the organisation. This was, in fact, a very low cost, dependable model compared with what many have done with outsourcing, which always results in higher costs as new people struggle to understand the infrastructure, coupled with less control as the organisation is no longer running things. Outsourcing coupled to the new DevOps model can be particularly expensive and, if the cloud is used, results in absolute loss of control of the core organisational and intellectual data. Whether Directors and Senior Managers think this is a good idea might depend upon their understanding of IT within the modern world.

However, even if things have been outsourced and have got into a real mess, it is, currently, still possible to buy the hardware components with which an in-house infrastructure may be built. Having done so, whatever technologies are deemed useful could be used and, if this infrastructure is built upon Linux, then costs may be kept very low. Indeed, if Open Source software is used throughout, then software costs could actually be kept to zero. The money saved, which would be very considerable indeed, could be used to employ and train in-house personnel. Now, *that* would represent an interesting proposition. Best of all, the PKI could be entirely designed, developed and maintained in-house. Self-signed certificates could be used for all internal purposes at no cost and, for outward-facing systems, third-party certificates from trusted certificate authorities could be used. A database for keeping track of all certificates and notifying support staff when they are due for renewal could easily be built with free, Open Source software. Make no mistake, the Open Source world offers software applications for almost any purpose you can think of and, if you cannot find something that already exists, you could build it yourself using Open Source development tools, a myriad of which are freely available. Some might hold that Open Source products cannot be as good as proprietary, closed source, paid for products. After all, how could a system which costs nothing be as good as one which costs $1.5m? The answer is, easily. In fact, the Open Source version will likely be easier to maintain, more stable and there will be far more information available, including within the many on-line forums.

And so, it absolutely remains viable to construct your own physical infrastructure and keep it either on-premise or in a custom-built data centre. Either way, once up and running, it will be relatively straightforward to maintain. Whether you would need to embrace the current fashion for 'DevOps' might depend upon your usage. However, if you understand your organisational business, there should be no need for frequent refreshing of your software applications, in which case, the DevOps philosophy is redundant. Albert Einstein once said that, if you cannot explain something in simple terms, then you don't understand it. Exactly. One might paraphrase this a little by saying that if you have to be constantly rebuilding your applications, then you don't understand your business, whether it be commercial, governmental or academic. So, the need for constant rebuilding and redeployment is somewhat questionable, to say the least. Details within the data might change, but this is not the same as application functionality which should not be changing anywhere near so frequently. With respect to PKI, there are many reasons why returning to an in-house, purpose-built infrastructure would be a good idea, most of which relate to ease of management which, in turn, translates to lower costs and better security. First of all, you know exactly where everything is. Where your certificates are stored and what their purpose is. This, in turn, makes them easy to account for and manage. Application-related certificates may be managed directly by the application support teams, as well as an overall view managed by a small, dedicated PKI function. Most certificate authorities have applications which will allow for the automated renewal of certificates supplied by them. This may be mirrored within your own PKI directory, with everything being kept up to date and functioning as it should. Comparison between this easy-to-maintain model and the cloud-based container and service mesh model is interesting. In theory, both should work fine with little hands on intervention required. In practice, with the latter model, you never really understand where things actually are and may consequently assume that everything is fine when, in reality, something may have been overlooked or, if totally automated, may simply never have been configured correctly in the first place, leaving you with a malfunctioning system. If this is the case, then a security risk also exists. Still, there may be advantages to such a model in certain situations. It is for the organisation concerned to decide.

In short, it is perfectly possible and feasible for a local, hardware-based infrastructure to be designed and built at a very low cost. Furthermore, there are good security reasons for doing things this way. Using in-house, properly trained staff also represents a good investment as, with proper management and guidance, it is likely that the organisation concerned will experience far fewer outages and, indeed, should have none at all. This, in turn, increases user confidence and represents good Public Relations (PR). Hardware costs are actually quite low in comparison with the charges being levied in order to maintain external infrastructures and software costs may be zero or very little indeed, if advantage is taken of the Open Source philosophy. In addition, while this would mean more people on the payroll, such costs are likely to be substantially less than that going out to third parties for managed infrastructures.

SUMMARY

In this chapter, it has been stressed that, for many organisations, it may still make a good deal of sense to manage their own, internal IT infrastructure, built along traditional methods and maintained accordingly. This would place everything back in their own hands and, with respect to a PKI, this is a very important and pertinent consideration. Managing a PKI properly is essential. With the larger numbers of certificates that a DevOps philosophy entails, that will, in many cases, mean turning to automation. However, turning to automation means losing control. Of course, you will have control over a centralised certificate management system (or someone else will on your behalf) but you will have little knowledge of where and when certificates are being created and destroyed, or whether they have been in accordance with a specific policy. Advocates will report that everything can be coded for within the various service meshes and, if need be, individual container templates; however, to do so means the creation of a hugely complex system overall. The likely end result would mean teams of (probably outsourced) coders doing things the way *they* think they should be done, but not necessarily in a coordinated manner. In any event, the organisation concerned will have lost direct control over the PKI and that is not a good thing. But there are other ways of going about things, as has been outlined within this chapter. Furthermore, when viewed from an ongoing cost perspective, these other ways may represent a huge saving.

Chapter 11

What happens when certificates expire?

What can go wrong?

For many years, it was common practice among IT support teams to configure self-signed certificates with long expiration dates. Sometimes, ten years, sometimes even up to 99 years. This was because they were considered something of a nuisance. They were useful to enable encrypted links between machines, but why over-complicate matters by necessitating regular renewals? Well, actually, there was a very good reason to place short renewal dates of one year, or perhaps two at the outside, and that was to force the teams concerned to constantly maintain a good understanding of what it was that they were supporting and why, including all the links with other applications and data sources, wherever they might be on the wider infrastructure. Similarly, with purchased certificates, it was a good thing to understand why they were purchased in the first place and whether that reason remained valid. Consequently, it would represent good practice to ensure that all certificates had a validity period of either one or two years. They could still be managed from a single directory or database, including triggers to notify support staff (at least two) a month or so before the expiration date.

There was also the question of support staff who might move to another department or, perhaps, even leave the organisation altogether. If they went, the knowledge of why these certificates were originally deployed would go with them and they would be forgotten about completely. Until, of course, they expired. Then, what would happen? Well, if they were simple web certificates or email certificates, users at the other end would simply receive messages stating that this web site or person cannot be trusted. This would hardly inspire confidence in the host organisation and may result in the loss of a customer or that particular web site being blocked by the receiving browser which would be very bad Public Relations (PR) for the web site–owning organisation. That would be bad enough, but things could get worse. If two machines regularly communicate via an encrypted link and, all of a sudden, that link stops because one of the certificates has expired, then it could simply break the link or, what may be worse, let the link continue in an unencrypted manner when no one understands that this is the case. This, in turn, exposes the organisation to an additional security risk. In the former scenario, things simply stop working and support staff will scratch their heads and wonder why (especially if they are an outsourced function) until someone, somewhere, remembers that there are such things as digital certificates and that they have a tendency to expire. If the link was to an external organisation, this could bring the host organisation's activities to a standstill, cause a lot of embarrassment and result in a loss of confidence from the other direction. This would represent very bad PR. In addition, valuable time will be wasted while the certificate authority concerned is contacted and the certificate renewed. Such things happen. At least, they do within organisations who do not really understand public key infrastructure (PKI) and how it works or how to best manage it.

Now, if you think about the scenarios referred to above and extrapolate this to a larger scale, with maybe thousands of machines and tens of thousands of certificates, then, as you might understand, the situation could become quite difficult. This would especially be the case if the IT function has been outsourced. Naturally, everything may be brought nicely back under control, if those concerned understand what is going on and act swiftly to remediate the situation.

As we can see from Figure 11.1, it is very easy to create certificates with long expiration dates but we should beware of the practice. Quite a number of IT failures and outages are actually due to expired certificates that nobody knew even existed. Finding these and replacing them may be a time-consuming process and, if there are a number of them involved, may cause lengthy outages which do much harm to an organisation's reputation and, for commercial organisations, may result in a significant loss of business, with the associated negative PR. However, it is surprisingly easy to get into such a situation, especially if an outsourced IT support team is looking after an infrastructure with which they are not familiar. In addition, such a team may or may not have a good understanding of PKI or where the certificate stores are on different operating systems and within specific applications. If a centralised PKI management system is being used, this may or may not have been kept up to date as developers sometimes just create certificates as a matter of routine, without particularly advising anyone else of their existence. They should, of course, be following a strictly enforced policy, but how often is this the case?

To give a particular example, imagine a database server which itself is residing upon a physical server (which might be a card with network-attached storage upon which the database software resides). First of all, the physical server will have certificates associated with it. Then, the database server will have certificates associated with it. Any client devices which are able to access the database, such as organisation laptops or desktops, will also have certificates. When a query is made to the database via one of the

Figure 11.1 Showing a self-signed certificate with long expiry date.

client devices, various certificates are referenced in order to identify the machines involved, undertake a cryptographic handshake and then encrypt the data as it passed across the network. There may be a dozen or so certificates involved in the overall process, from issuing the query, running it on the database server, retrieving the data from storage and sending it over the network to the client. If any of these certificates fail, then the transaction will fail. If this connection is going outside the organisational network and accessing a third-party resource, then there are more certificates involved, including those from a trusted certificate authority. But once again, if a certificate fails (through being out of date), then the transaction will likely fail or, worse, leave you exposed from a security perspective. There may be a fallback position of data passing in plain text, but this is hardly acceptable and, to make matters worse, you may not even realise that it is happening.

If, as a part of your organisation's daily business, you make dozens of such requests, or maybe hundreds, or even thousands, then your PKI had better be in a good state of health. This desirable state is easily achieved if a small, specialist team is employed to actively manage the PKI. If we consider the current situation whereby everyone suddenly seems to have acquired a passion for the DevOps model and the use of containers, service meshes and all the associated paraphernalia, then it becomes all the more necessary to really understand your certificate estate. This includes an understanding of how containers work, how communications are undertaken with 'sidecars' and 'service meshes' where the certificates are stored, when they are due to expire and so on. Within a large organisation, this may be no small matter. If you don't really understand it, then you cannot effectively support it or troubleshoot it when something goes wrong. And something will, most definitely, go wrong. When it does, you need to be able to respond quickly and put things right. This speed of operation is an oft-quoted benefit of the container model, but will it work in this scenario? The answer is yes, probably, at least, if you have installed all the right components, including for telemetry purposes, and, if you have installed them correctly (in which case why did it fail?) and if you know exactly where everything is situated.

Even assuming the above, there may be two dozen developers who have worked on code to be placed on the aforementioned servers. There may equally be a dozen or so third-party software solutions which have been added since the database was conceived and built (and who was the acting Chief Architect?) Any one of which may have had a negative impact. Ah! I hear you say, "but with DevOps", you can replace the errant container almost immediately. But that infers that you will know exactly where the failure is, and it could be almost anywhere and take you hours to discover. Then, you will need to understand where the faulty code is and identify specific certificates. Multiply this situation by 100, and as you will see, you will have real problems finding and replacing the failed certificates. Even worse, if the systems have not failed completely, then you will have quite a job finding and checking all the certificates. Now, multiply the issue by tens of thousands and, as might be anticipated, we now have a real problem on our hands.

The other question, which has been touched upon briefly, is the precise location of certificates. When an application is first installed and configured, things like certificate addresses are understood and located accordingly by the specific team concerned. However, if anything should move, an i.p. address changed perhaps, or maybe the application scaled up and moved onto different servers, then some of these certificates may become orphaned. The problem is, the support team involved may not be aware of the fact. They may have re-configured or re-issued some certificates, but there is always the possibility, if not probability, that some may slip through the net. This is where having an up-to-date inventory of all certificates, what their purpose is and where they are located, is so important. Without such an inventory, how can the application support team, or new DevOps team, possibly understand the broader situation? The answer is that they cannot. And so things break and outages occur. On a large, sophisticated organisational network, this can become a serious issue. If, at the same time, IT staff are being outsourced, then it is twice the issue. If, in addition, the organisation is moving to a microservices-based architecture, then it is twice the issue again, or more. We simply cannot afford to ignore the role that a PKI plays within any organisational IT infrastructure, especially if some, or all of it, resides in the cloud.

In particular, we must understand the implications of certificates being in the wrong place or expiring. This issue also occurs within a dual or multiple O/S infrastructure which, these days, is the norm rather than the exception. It used to be problematic enough when support teams would wrestle with the inconsistencies between Windows, Linux and Mainframes. But now, we have a proliferation of Apple Mac laptops and mobile devices, plus a range of Android-based tablets and mobile devices. All of these are required to connect into the main organisational network, sometimes on-campus, sometimes from known remote locations and sometimes from untrusted public networks. All such eventualities need to be catered for and every device concerned will need a certificate on it. When it connects and a handshake is undertaken, certificates will need to be checked, and for this to occur, we must, of course, understand where to find them and, when we do, recognise them as being issued either by our organisation or to our organisation (or an external organisation) by a trusted certificate authority. Within the servers, desktops and laptops of our own organisation, we shall need to know the location of all of the standard certificate stores, as used by the operating systems, as well as that of any application-specific certificate stores. And, it goes without saying, that we need to understand which certificates are where. And this must be the case for every single certificate used by our organisational IT infrastructure, even if there are thousands of them.

If any part of this broader understanding is left wanting, then an unnecessary risk is being run which might, one day, bring down at least part of our IT infrastructure. When it does, the ability of support staff to get it up and running again within a reasonable time frame will depend very much upon who they are and what development models are being pursued. We witness this all too often within the modern world, especially when trying to interface to public systems. The excuse, "its not our fault, the IT is down" has become commonplace. It did not use to be this way. All of this should be taken into consideration when planning or running an IT infrastructure. And PKI underpins almost all of it, one way or another.

SUMMARY

In this chapter, the possibility of things going wrong when certificates expire has been considered, together with the possible causes of difficulty when trying to put things right. It is not just the issue of expiring certificates that one must consider, but the question of why it is that they have expired without being noticed. Mostly, this will be because their exact whereabouts were unknown, maybe even their existence in the first place. This would not happen within a properly run PKI. However, this is why this book has been written, in order to point out the dangers awaiting those who do not pay proper attention to PKI and, in the DevOps model especially, this is a very easy situation in which to find oneself. Every day, we hear of more IT 'outages'. How can this be, if the propaganda being waged by the technology suppliers is correct?

Chapter 12

How do we ensure that certificates do not expire?

Methodologies for security

It is clear, from the previous chapter, that any organisation can get into a real mess if certificates start to expire, if they have been forgotten about or, perhaps, simply have been placed in the wrong location. It is equally clear that, under the DevOps model, this situation is exacerbated and may easily lead to a great deal of wasted time and associated cost. Consequently, we must strive to keep things on an even keel and ensure that our management of the public key infrastructure (PKI), and all that this entails, is absolutely correct.

The first step must surely be to appoint a dedicated PKI team who, even if their knowledge is not initially complete, may be trained to the point of being first-class PKI practitioners. This need not be a large team. Indeed, three or four individuals will be enough to provide contingency due to leave or illness. Their primary responsibility will be as the source of expertise for PKI. They will be the team that the other teams turn to for advice. They, in turn, will educate the other teams in order to ensure that they are following best practice with respect to the organisational PKI. If an overall PKI management system is being employed, it is the PKI team who will be trained on the use of this system and it will be they alone who have administer rights over the system. All requests for externally sourced certificates will come through this team and will be approved, or denied, by them alone. Furthermore, the deployed architecture of the management system will be designed, approved and built by this team. They will understand exactly how the management system interacts with every other system within the broader network. If other systems and service layers need to interact with the PKI management system, it will be the PKI expert team who design and orchestrate this interaction. They will then instruct other teams how to make use of it. Whatever the purveyors of these other systems and layers suggest, it will be the PKI team who have the final say in everything appertaining to PKI. Others shall have to do design their own offerings around the PKI model, not the other way around. This last point is crucially important to understand. It is the PKI that is the most important entity, not the services and layers who might be using it. It is primarily for this reason that the organisation requires such a dedicated PKI team.

The skills required by this specialist team must be broad-based IT skills, preferably won by experience within the organisation. They must understand both Windows, Linux and, increasingly, Apple operating systems and where the associated keystores are generally held. They must also understand mainframes and the applications which are running upon them. In addition, they must come to terms with the new DevOps methodology and all of the technologies used within this broader, cloud-based framework. This might seem like a tall order, but it is entirely realistic for such a team to grasp all of this and to understand it in its entirety. This is why they need to be a dedicated team. One thing that an organisation should absolutely not do is to outsource this function. It must be managed in-house by your own personnel. This is very important, and it will represent a decision which, in the end, will save the organisation a great deal of time. money and embarrassment due to IT-related outages. PKI is the foundation upon which your IT framework is built. If it is wrong or becomes broken, your IT will be broken, with all the consequences that this entails.

Now, let us explore some of the understanding that this specialist PKI team must absorb. Firstly, they must understand the various certificate standards that exist. Mostly, they will be dealing with those of the x.509 persuasion, but there are others. They must understand every field within these certificates, how and why they might be used and when to use them. Also, how to check them and how to recognise what it is they are seeing. They must also understand how certificate authorities and registration authorities work, what they are and what they do. And, of course, they must understand the concepts which lie at the core of a PKI, how it works and what is required in order to enable it. Then, they must apply this knowledge to their own organisation, thinking through how certificates will work and when and where they should be used. From here, they will need to construct an organisation-specific policy for the use of a PKI. This should be in the form of a clear and concise document which sets out precisely how certificates should be used within this particular organisation and the IT infrastructure which it supports. This will include roles and responsibilities of all personnel who might possibly be involved, from those in purchasing negotiating with certificate authorities to those writing code for deployment either as services or applications and, in particular, those adopting the role of system architect. How each of these and others who might be involved are to liaise with the specialist PKI team will also be described, clearly and unambiguously, leaving absolutely no doubt as to who is responsible for what. This might seem like an obvious requirement, and yet, it is surprising just how many organisations don't even get this important first step right. If it is not right, then it is wrong and the resulting PKI will likely soon become fragmented, badly organised and set firmly upon the road to failure. This statement of roles and responsibilities might also be described within an organisational chart which, in turn, might be deployed upon the organisation's internal web site or wiki, from where it may easily be referenced. A copy might usefully be mounted and placed on the wall where the PKI team work, as a reminder to all those concerned. This would help to explain things to new IT personnel as they appear on the scene.

Having created and distributed this organisational policy, the PKI team must then make it their business to understand the complete infrastructure, where certificates are usually stored within different operating systems (and versions of operating systems) and where application-specific certificates exist. This understanding must additionally embrace any new development work being undertaken and every model being used for development. This is not a small task, and it will require a good deal of keenly focused effort. Another map may be produced which clearly states where the default certificate stores exist in every case. This document will be linked to the policy document. What they will quickly discover is that there are exceptions. Lots of them. Mostly application-specific and sometimes because strict development methodologies and recommendations have not been followed.

In addition, they will likely find that individuals have acquired certificates without advising anyone else. These will often be simple email certificates but, sometimes, an individual may have more than one, valid at the same time, perhaps because they have forgotten the password associated with the original certificate. Discovering all of these things will require some pure detective work. Individuals will need to be quizzed and, every time an email message is spotted as being signed or encrypted, then the PKI 'detectives' must quickly get on the case and understand where this certificate has come from. If there is more than one certificate associated with an individual, then this must be rationalised, leaving just one, clearly defined certificate associated with that name. Other certificates must be destroyed, if they were self-signed, or revoked, if they have been issued by a certificate authority. Managing this task over what might be several thousand employees will be a large undertaking. However, once completed, and with a single user certificate properly logged in the certificate database for each individual who needs one, the ongoing picture may be much more easily managed.

This brings us nicely to the subject of education and awareness. Understandably, those personnel not involved in IT matters will likely have little or no knowledge of PKI and certificate management. Indeed, a great many within the IT area may have little knowledge of the same, depending upon their precise role. However, it is important that all personnel have at least a basic, working knowledge of PKI theory and why they have certificates, either personally, or associated with an application which they might use regularly. It follows then that a PKI awareness raising campaign must be designed, configured and orchestrated within the organisation. This is time consuming and must be fitted in somehow in parallel with all of the other tasks awaiting the PKI team. However, it must be undertaken if an organisation is to gain, and maintain control over its PKI, whatever the infrastructure being employed. One may start to understand just why such a dedicated PKI team is crucially important to the organisation or enterprise. There is much for them to do and the workload will never cease. It might change complexion now and again, but it will always be there, and without a dedicated team to administer it, things will quickly become a mess, as has happened in so many instances lately. Furthermore, if you are thinking of changing your development methodology to something akin to the microservices and DevOps model, then you most certainly require such a dedicated team.

The awareness raising programme itself will require proper documentation. It is likely that the PKI team will undertake a series of presentations or lectures, maybe even the odd conference attendance, but this is meaningless unless supported by proper documentation which may be referenced by a broad cross-section of individuals, from IT support staff to business managers, senior managers and, especially, directors, all of whom need to understand the broader situation. In parallel, this will teach them much about their own IT infrastructure which they probably did not previously understand. It is essential that the entire organisation is covered by this awareness raising programme. It only takes one little misunderstanding, somewhere, to cause significant PKI-related problems.

When the awareness raising is complete, the certificate database built, populated and checked, the infrastructure properly documented, and in fine detail, and everything checked, and then checked again, then it will be possible for the PKI team to take a step backwards and observe what is happening in practice. Hopefully, they will find that policies are being adhered to, roles and responsibilities respected and working practices followed implicitly. Anything less than this will not be good enough. If loopholes are found, or if development personnel are taking short cuts and not doing things properly, this must be jumped on immediately and sorted out. With PKI, an organisation simply cannot tolerate sloppiness or individuals doing things their way, in defiance of agreed policy. This is how things go wrong. If we wish to ensure that certificates do not expire, with all that such expiration entails, and are only issued in strict accordance with in-place policy, then we must exert a tight control over the organisational PKI. It is black and white. There is no grey area here.

Having understood where every single certificate is and why it is there, we may now log them all within our certificate database or centralised management system, noting their properties and, importantly, their expiration dates. A logical way to manage them from here is to have at least two contacts listed, together with their email addresses and telephone numbers, for every certificate. Typically, these contacts will be working within the application support teams for each affected application. When a certificate comes within a month of expiration, an automated email message may be sent to both contacts, asking for a response and an assurance that the certificate has been renewed, together with the details of the new certificate. When a response is received, the certificate database may be updated as appropriate. If a response is not received within one week, another message will be automatically sent to the two named contacts. If another week passes, another message is sent, and this one will be repeated now every day. However, by the time this point is reached, the PKI team will have taken matters into their own hands. Firstly, they will investigate why a response has not been received. Have both of these named individuals left the department or the organisation? If they are still within the organisation, they will be tracked down and asked why they did not update the PKI team accordingly. And then, two new individuals will be given responsibility for the certificates in question, and the PKI team will assist them in renewing the certificates before they expire. Mostly, it won't come to this point as responsible individuals will remain in place and will respond to the first message received, updating the certificates in question and supplying details of the new or updated certificates. Having some sort of automation like this in place is essential when dealing with large numbers of certificates.

In the DevOps world, there is an expectation that an automated certificate authority will simply issue certificates as needed and destroy them when not required, as containers are built, deployed and then destroyed. This may work with self-signed certificates, up to a point, but it would be dangerous to simply rely on this mechanism and assume that everything is working fine when, in reality, you simply don't know, as you have no direct control over the process. If something goes wrong and, inevitably, it will, the first you will know about it is when a process fails because a communication handshake failed, but it might take you a while to discover this. Indeed, the containers involved may have already been replaced with altered versions which appear to be working. These sort of failures will be hard to discover and put right in close to real time. More often than not, an outage of some sort will occur because the 'automated' certificate issuing process has missed something or has simply not been referenced, or versioning has got into a mess. This model may work fine with a contained number of nodes or containers, but when we start reaching tens of thousands of nodes, which is entirely realistic in many cases, then it is dangerous to assume that they are all going to be working seamlessly with this automated certificate authority. Note that there is a distinction here between automated calls to a conventional certificate authority and the construction and implementation of an automated service designed to interface with all the microservice nodes or containers within your application space. When this application space is the cloud, you can magnify this problem a hundred fold. This issue illustrates why the entire application development and usage model of any organisation must be very carefully considered and mapped out in advance. Key to this understanding will be an equal understanding of the important role that a PKI plays within this picture. If this understanding is not in place, then the organisation in question remains vulnerable.

SUMMARY

In this chapter, it has been shown that the primary way in which to prevent the expiration of certificates is simply good organisation. In the Middle Kingdom, the ancient Egyptians, under the rule of both the Senruset and Amenemhat dynasties, understood, perhaps better than anyone before or since, the importance of bringing order from chaos. They knew that it took as much, if not more, time and effort to produce chaos, as it does to maintain order. So why not have order? With order comes a confidence that things are going to work as expected. Senruset and Amenemhat understood this well and ensured that all things prospered under their guidance. And they *really* prospered. Our PKI specialist teams need to take a similar approach. Yes, it will be difficult at times, but effort is rewarded with success and the confidence that things are being managed properly. From this, an ever more detailed map of the IT estate and all the certificates within it may be produced. We have shown, in this section, that a certificate database may be constructed and automated in order to send out messages prior to certificate expiration, in order that those responsible may respond and ensure that there are no outages due to certificate expiration. For the ancient Egyptians, undertaking this task well would have been a matter of pride. The PKI team need to instil such a pride in all those responsible for certificates. Then, we shall have order. Then, things shall work. And there shall be no outages. No chaos.

Chapter 13

How does the human interaction work?

Managing things manually

In the brave new world of microservices, kubernetes, service meshes, code repositories and all the other paraphernalia that we were once surviving quite happily without, automation has become a key requisite of being able to operate within that model. This will be seen by most as a convenience, by some as an absolute necessity and by others simply as the way that things are done today. Within industry generally, automation has led to ever-growing profits among a smaller number of companies within each sector, coupled to mass redundancies, unemployment and the de-skilling of generations. What passes now for skills, in any sector, is usually just a very basic knowledge of support issues, while the real knowledge is held by an increasingly small number of individuals who have been privileged enough to enjoy a proper education which has taught them the distinction between qualifications and understanding. This minority represent those who actually design the future by the products and services being generated within their particular sector. Unfortunately, another missing ingredient in modern times is moral courage. This lack of decency and living to an honourable code results in the development of technologies which no one really needs, except those who are generating obscene profits which they don't know what to do with, while others live in misery. The IT industry is a leader in this respect as what it generates affects the lives of many millions, either directly or indirectly and rarely for the better. The author noticed an interesting statistic while visiting an optician recently. It stated how in excess of 60% of all primary school children in my country were now suffering from short sightedness. I was shocked at this revelation, but hardly surprised as they are glued to mobile phones, tablets and TVs for the majority of their waking hours. They are also experiencing increasing problems of attention span, social interaction and the ability to learn and understand. The term 'learning difficulties' has become almost ubiquitous, and you will not have to look very far to find someone within your immediate community who is thus tagged. What used

DOI: 10.1201/9781003360674-13

to be a rare exception is now almost expected. This is a clear example of technology positively harming generations of humans while making obscene profits for a few. Furthermore, the supposed benefits of such technologies are far outweighed by the harm that they bring. A human being is far more precious than any technology.

And so, it is within IT. We have long since passed the point at which it could be said to be truly useful to the majority that use it. Again, the supposed benefits are outweighed by the destruction of human interaction and initiative. Look at what has happened with the banks and energy suppliers as an example. Has this resulted in lower costs for the consumer? No, quite the opposite. From the organisational perspective, operating costs have gone up roughly in line with the level and intensity of IT deployment. In addition, such deployment has led to unemployment and a skills shortage beyond the wildest imagination. The wise organisation will therefore look long and hard before adopting any new IT-related technology. Of course, they will be under intense pressure from suppliers who will say and do anything in order to convince the organisation that they must adopt the latest trends. There is an 'Emperor's new clothes' syndrome here which is hard to ignore. If all else fails, bribery and corruption are always ready to hand, especially within the public sector, and they are used without hesitation.

Getting back to public key infrastructure (PKI), it is important to understand the reality of the above made observations, in order to design your organisation's approach to implementing and maintaining a proper PKI. There are companies and services who will proudly maintain that they will simply take everything out of your hands, in order that you need not worry about it. That would be a very big mistake, especially if such companies are using the cloud. That is not to say that such a service couldn't or wouldn't work. It might well work, at least for a while. But this is a one-way street. Having gone down such a road, there is no turning back as, now, you would have lost all control over your own PKI. Consequently, the cost of bringing it all back in-house would be enormous and most accounting departments would not sanction such a move. The same company might well be able to sell you a software management system which you could run yourselves. This would be better, depending upon the complexity and cost of such an approach. You might find that the learning curve is a good deal steeper than anticipated. Or, you could simply build your own certificate database and design the policies around its use in-house, taking advantage of specialist knowledge within the organisation. This would be better still.

Even with your own, custom-built certificate database, there remains the question of what would be sensible to automate and what would be better left in the hands of trusted individuals. This question should be addressed right at the start, before the database is built, and input should be taken from both development and support staff before a policy document is finally drawn up. This, in turn, will inform the design specification of the database. Items for consideration might usefully include the following:

- The procedure for creating and registering a self-signed digital certificate.
- The procedure for requesting an external certificate from a certificate authority.
- The precise specification for all types of certificate that might be required.
- The central repository for all such information.
- The process for sending out renewal reminders.
- The required response to such reminders.
- How the certificate database is populated.
- How new certificates are discovered on the network.
- Roles and responsibilities of all concerned.

Discussing such matters openly with the development and support personnel will provide an insight as to how things are currently working. For example, UNIX/LINUX developers will have well-defined ideas about how they manage certificates. Support staff may or may not understand where the certificate stores are on different client machines and servers, but they may be familiar with the consequences of failing certificates. In any event, such discussions will be illuminating. It will probably be found that there are a number of spreadsheets containing lists of issued certificates, but these could be anywhere, including being buried within a developer's private folder structure that only he can access. If this is the case, the retrieval and examination of these spreadsheets will be a worthwhile step towards developing a broader understanding, even if they are not entirely in synchronisation. If the organisation has been used to an application-specific model, whereupon certain individuals are aligned with an application both before and after development, then they will also have a good understanding of how the certificates associated with that particular application are working. They probably issued most, if not all of them, themselves and will know where they are and what sort of expiration lengths have been used. This is also a very good place to start for the PKI team.

Once such discussions have taken place and the PKI team have a reasonable understanding of the certificate estate and how it has been managed to date, they may then start to write policies around how things will work into the future. These policies will include the certificate store locations to be used on different platforms, how certificates are logged and the processes for requesting and deploying them. Such policies, themselves, provide a unifying influence which is a good thing and is a good place from where to start the next phase of construction and management.

Almost certainly, it will be necessary to construct a centralised certificate database which may be updated in real time and backed up nightly. This may either be quite a simple flat file database in a common format such as dBase, which may be read by almost any application, including the popular spreadsheets, as found in all the popular office suites. Alternatively, it may be a more sophisticated database using SQL queries and deployed according to a client–server model, or it may be an LDAP (Lightweight Directory Access Protocol) directory, optimised for fast searches. The choice of database might depend upon how many certificates are anticipated, what their expiry periods will typically be and what degree of automation might be required. An advantage of LDAP is that it is an open specification, and there are many Open Source directory servers that are readily available, proven and cost nothing (unless you wish to purchase some sort of support package which, in most cases, will be unnecessary). A good example of the latter is the ApacheDS, which is written in JAVA and may therefore be embedded into custom applications if required. It has in-built support for Kerberos as well as password policy support. It is also cross-platform and may run on Windows or LINUX servers and there is a good community associated with it. However, ApacheDS is simply one of many such LDAP servers. There equally exists a number of conventional Open Source database applications, a notable one being PostgreSQL, which has been around, in one way or another, for over 30 years and has a large following. However, this follows a fully relational database model and may be more sophisticated than you need. Probably, you will decide that a good directory server, against which you may write standardised queries and receive back fast results, even with high numbers of entries, may fit the bill. Such a model would also support a mild degree of automation via easy to maintain scripts.

The primary purpose of your certificate management database will be to list every certificate that you issue, with fields for type, issuing authority, at least two support individuals and, importantly, the start and end dates of the validity period. You may then write queries in order to check expiry dates and, before they are due, notify the listed support personnel by email, sending a copy to the PKI central team. A mechanism for the supporting personnel to confirm renewal and update the details of the new certificate should be provided. The directory may then allow the original certificate to expire gracefully. The precise details will depend upon the earlier discussions and related policies, but something akin to that described will probably be what you decide upon.

Note that, with the model articulated above, there remains a good deal of human interaction. This is crucially important for various reasons, among which is the fact that it will keep all of those concerned fully aware of the organisational PKI, how it works and what sort of problems can arise when things go wrong. Consequently, if things do go wrong, and they shouldn't, the team will easily be able to identify the problem and deal with it quickly. The organisation will benefit from a high degree of in-house knowledge and a support team second to none. These days, such skills are priceless and, if lost, are very hard to regain. Furthermore, as may be derived from the above discussion, it is a relatively easy matter to tackle PKI properly and put in place a very good, in-house capability which would not be possible to replicate with outsourced suppliers. Consequently, the organisation keeps control of a vital mechanism which underpins almost every interaction with the outside world as well as providing internal network security. It really is not that difficult if a measured, well-considered approach is taken.

An alternative to the above-mentioned methodology is to buy in a purpose-built, commercial PKI centralised management system. This will have similar functionality to that previously mentioned but might include a higher degree of automation, including certificate discovery. On paper, this will all sound like a marvellous idea and, no doubt, the suppliers will be able to provide screen shots of the system in operation, which will look most impressive. What will be less impressive will be the cost, which is likely to be very high, the complexity of installation and deployment, which will be significant, the training required for operators and, most of all, the reality that this will be a closed system for which you will be obliged to pay even more for a support package of some sort. Furthermore, there will be limitations around numbers of certificates, operators and so on, all of which will point towards spiralling costs. The assumed or otherwise implied assurance that this will solve all of your PKI-related issues will be difficult to realise in practice. In reality, it may just further complicate what was already a complicated picture. Such an approach may or may not work for your organisation, but tread carefully, the price you pay will be more than you expected and you will lose the lower level skills which are so important.

It will be no surprise to learn that there are also a number of Open Source developments which provide, if not a complete management system, various components which may easily be linked together in order to build one. This would represent a good approach for an organisation which is already Open Source oriented and which has a number of competent, in-house developers, conversant with the various Open Source standards and developments. The issue with this approach is that, if care is not taken, one may easily end up with a 'Frankenstein's monster' of a design which might be difficult to support, especially if development personnel move on to other organisations. Nevertheless, this remains a valid option and will have the associated benefit of developing in-house skills and related expertise. If a fairly sophisticated system is considered necessary, it may certainly be built from carefully selected Open Source components. Once again, care is necessary in the selection of these components. Some of them come and go without reaching maturity.

On reflection, the first approach discussed herein would be the best for the majority of organisations. It would keep things simple from a technical perspective, and thus easily supportable, while ensuring a strong human interaction within your organisation. This, in turn, means the development of specialist skills, coupled to a complete in-house understanding of where everything is and why. Most importantly, it would also ensure that, should things go awry, the necessary skills to put things right are immediately available. Furthermore, in real terms, it would prove to be the least expensive approach in almost every case. In IT, human interaction is highly desirable. For the management of an organisational PKI, it is essential.

SUMMARY

In this section, different approaches to managing a PKI have been examined, with a particular emphasis on human interaction. This is important for the understanding of a corporate or organisational PKI, and not just the PKI itself, but everything that it touches which, in most cases, will be your entire operation, as well as those of others. While it is increasingly possible to automate many, if not all, of the related tasks, it has been shown that, for various reasons, this may not be a good idea. Preserve human interaction and you preserve knowledge of one of the most important factors underpinning almost every transaction and interaction undertaken by your operation. Consequently, it makes very good sense to do so. Unfortunately, for far too many, the opposite is also true.

Chapter 14

Can we organise everything ourselves?

Understanding what to do

The short answer to the primary question posed by the title of this chapter is yes. Yes, we can organise everything ourselves and, furthermore, it is a very good idea to do so. But let us start right at the beginning. When the term 'Information Technology' was first coined, it was not considered as a mechanism with which to give away all of your precious organisational or commercial data to third parties whom you don't know anything about, or even which continent your data and intellectual property will end up in. And yet, for many government agencies and commercial enterprises, this is precisely what has happened. Another analogy which was made in the early days of IT was that of your operational data being the life blood of your organisation. Indeed, so where is the sense of giving it away to third parties while paying them vast amounts of money for the privilege of doing so? For most, there surely is none. In addition, almost every government agency, commercial enterprise or academic institution who has done this started off with their own, perfectly good internal IT infrastructure, administered by their own, perfectly capable IT personnel. In other words, they already had all of this capability safely in-house, so where was the sense in paying to transfer this into a third-party's hands? There surely was none. There were other immoral mechanisms at play here, the result of which was the creation of chaos out of order. The ancient Egyptians would never have allowed such a situation to persist. In relation to all such matters, we should ask a very simple question. Just one word. One of the smallest in the dictionary, but one of the most powerful words in the English language. Just three little letters. And that word is 'why?' For every suggestion, for every idea, ask the question why? And, if there is not a very good answer, don't do it. This is the basis of science. Question everything. And then question again, and keep questioning as you go. If IT is recognised as a science, then we should surely apply a scientific rigour to it. But this is simply not happening in our brave new world of IT.

So where should we start in asking such questions? Right at the top. At director or ministerial level. And the questions should not be around which of the new technologies to use, but should go right back to the principles of managing operational information, including the processing of information

DOI: 10.1201/9781003360674-14

entrusted to us by our clients. There are additional questions of integrity, honour and accountability which should also be to the fore within any such discussions. And so, gaining control of the organisational public key infrastructure (PKI) might become a useful first step in regaining control over the broader IT landscape. Furthermore, for most, there are very good reasons why such a direction would be beneficial. The first question then is, given the importance of a PKI to everything that we do, should we bring this back under direct control using our own internal human resources? For most, the answer to this question should be yes. In which case, it will be necessary to identify precisely which human resources will be necessary to bring this about. The desirability of a specialist PKI team has already been mentioned and this should be pencilled in as the first step. But who should they be? Well, if we assume that, for a middle-sized operation, a small team of four or five should suffice, then, the next step is to identify the skills that this small team should encompass. It goes without saying that they should all have a competent understanding of PKI, both the principles and the actuality of operation. At least two of them should complement this set of skills with an equal understanding of application development and be conversant with current standards in this context. Note, that there is a distinction between standards and methodologies. The former constitute a useful set of rules which ensure compatibility. The latter are reflected mostly in currently fashionable approaches which may or may not stand the test of time. Most of them don't. At least, one member of this PKI team should additionally have solid marketing skills and should be capable of interaction at all levels within the organisation.

Having defined the skills required within the specialist PKI team, attention may be drawn to the other human resources that will be required in order to complete the picture. These will include in-house application development skills, together with an associated support function which encompasses not just PKI, but operating systems, networks, security and, where appropriate, distinct application support functions, at least for the primary applications which define your operation. If organised properly, this need not be a large number of individuals and may be tailored very closely to the actual requirements of the operation, at least as far as a PKI and security is concerned. It may be grown over time to encompass other elements as considered necessary. The irony is that most organisations used to have these in-house skills, but let them go because the accountants were worried about liabilities, in particular, the desirability of an organisation-specific pension plan and, of course whatever national obligations were in place, together with the financial contributions required to meet them. Many have since discovered that the sum of all such obligations pales into insignificance compared to the sums being paid out to third-party application and support providers. Furthermore, in the latter case, all control over the organisation's IT assets and, therefore, their specific intellectual property is lost completely. Many have discovered that, with hindsight, it really made no sense at all to follow such a model. But now, with the advent of the cloud, microservices, containers and all the rest, they are doing it all over again. Whether this makes any sense at all for your organisation is something that only you can decide. However, such a decision should be an informed one, based upon solid scientific principles, and one which is only taken at the highest levels.

Let us assume for a moment that the decision to manage the PKI entirely in-house has been taken. We have defined the skills required by the specialist PKI team who will orchestrate the activity and bring it to fruition. They will also manage it on an ongoing basis once it is established. We have additionally accepted that a number of other in-house resources shall be required, together with an appreciation of the skill sets involved. However, we shall, to a certain extent, be relying upon the PKI team to precisely define these skills and identify the numbers of individuals required. Consequently, the first step is to recruit the specialist PKI team. This is where the human resources department may step in and arrange for the connection with appropriate agencies, advertising or both, in order to get the right sort of individuals walking through the door. However, interviewing and recruiting should not be left to the human resources (HR) department alone. They may certainly be responsible for creating a short list but, once such a list is created, interviews should be conducted by a small team of directors, chosen for their understanding of how the organisation actually operates. This is important as the understanding needs to flow in both directions. Prospective employees need to understand the organisational philosophy and how it is put into practice, and the directors need to gain an understanding, not only of the competence of prospective employees, but how well they fit with this organisational philosophy. The HR department is simply not equipped for such an undertaking. They never are, and this is why we often end up with the wrong people in the wrong positions. Managed properly, this process should not be too onerous and the specialist PKI team may quickly be put in place. Once in position and acclimatised to the organisation philosophy, they may now set upon the task of drawing up the draft operational policies while simultaneously taking stock of the available IT-related human resources. Within a matter of a very few weeks, they should be in a position to report back to management with a properly drawn up, well-defined plan, detailing all of the associated requirements. This, in turn, may be quickly considered, modified if and where applicable, and then signed off for actuation. Bearing in mind that there will be some sort of historic certificate management in place which will also need to be understood in depth. Now, the PKI team can really get to grips with the situation.

Having ensured that all the necessary in-house personnel are now in place, they can be properly trained and made aware of the PKI plan of action, while becoming conversant with the associated policies and rules of engagement. Within the PKI team, those responsible for development will have, by now, constructed a certificate database which may now be populated both directly from within the team and by the other related personnel who would have been carefully identified. The queries and scripts necessary for sending out automated reminders may be built and tested, with simple interfaces designed in order to make it easy to add personnel as and when required. Similarly, a simple interface with which development and support staff may interrogate systems for certificates, or request new certificates, may also be designed and tested. Thus, we shall have maintained human interaction while making it a simple matter to provide for it.

Attention may then be focused upon the application level, noting where certificates are used and why, where they are stored and other important information. In each case, the presence of a certificate should be questioned. Who or what is referencing that particular certificate and for what purpose? If such a question may not be satisfactorily answered, then the certificate may not be necessary. That little question 'why?' should be asked at every opportunity during this certificate discovery stage. What we shall be left with is a well-documented list containing every certificate usefully being used within the enterprise. This will be embedded into our certificate database from where all such certificates will now be managed. The developers and application support personnel may, in the meantime, be absorbing the appropriate policies which will shape all future certificate issuance requests. They will get into the habit of following these policies and procedures and will, consequently, by default, be building an equally sound knowledge of all the systems and services which, together, constitute the IT infrastructure of the organisation concerned. With this ever-increasing knowledge comes the ability to take back in-house the support of all major applications and systems. Even if some of these have been put in the cloud, it will still be possible to understand what they are, how they are running and what infrastructural requirements they have. It will then be possible to replicate this infrastructure on in-house hardware, establish each system on it, check all the connectivity, including certificates and then, finally, cut over to the in-house system. After this has been operating successfully for a defined period of time, the cloud-based version may be decommissioned. If the organisation were to do this for all of its primary systems, it would slowly regain control of its own IT operation. And *that* would be a very good thing indeed. Needless to say, the PKI will have an important role to play in such an initiative and will, in fact, be the catalyst for the change that is needed in order to regain control, as the PKI will effectively be the map of all transactions and interactions between systems. And so, taking such steps under the banner of PKI may well represent salvation for the organisation concerned and its particular collection of IT assets.

At the application level, it is a simple matter to discover how the application is functioning and what dependencies it has. From here, a list of functioning certificates and their properties is easily derived. This, in turn, may be verified with the central PKI team who may now bring that particular application into the central PKI database. Replicate this activity around the organisation and we shall quickly and effectively be in a position to organise everything ourselves. Better still, we shall be building a framework of knowledge which will enable us to systematically regain control over our IT estate, application by application. It is all quite simple if one follows an ordered approach. Furthermore, the benefits will multiply as we go, resulting in a more knowledgeable, happier IT staff who, in turn, will be providing an enhanced service to the organisation, whose costs, in real terms, will have reduced. That would seem like a worthwhile state of affairs.

SUMMARY

In this chapter, we have reaffirmed the possibility of not only managing an organisational PKI in-house, but organising everything needed to do this ourselves. It is simply a matter of building the right skill set. Managing the PKI down to application level provides us with the concurrent capability to build this skill set, even beyond what is necessary for PKI. Indeed, it enables us to rebuild our IT skills to the point where the organisation may easily regain control of its IT estate and associated assets, working to an organised and structured plan in order to do so. Furthermore, the software tools required with which to bring about this desirable state of affairs are almost all freely available under the Open Source model which, in turn, promotes a further development of skills.

Chapter 15

How long does it take to implement a proper PKI?

Understanding the scale of the problem

The chaotic picture referred to above is by no means uncommon. In fact, it is probably the norm. However, there is no reason why things may not be transformed from such a position to one of order. The first step is having the will to implement a public key infrastructure (PKI) properly. This can only come from senior management within the organisation. It is a matter of corporate or organisational philosophy. Once established, it is an easy matter to draw up a plan for execution; this whole process might take just a couple of weeks. Then, it will be necessary to recruit the specialist PKI team. Understanding what qualifications are desirable and, importantly, the knowledge level of systems such as those used by your organisation, might take a week or so of discussion and research, followed by two or three weeks of interviewing and selecting those who will form the specialist team. By now, a couple of months may have elapsed, and it might seem that little progress is being made but, in fact, important progress will have been made as the groundwork will have been put in place ready for the project itself.

When the PKI expert team is in place, they will need to spend a few weeks familiarising themselves with the IT infrastructure while simultaneously drawing up policies and instructions for those in the development and application support areas. When they feel ready to do so, probably after a month, they may initiate an awareness and education programme, to be run in every department. This programme will run right through from the basic principles of a PKI to precisely how it will be implemented within the organisation and by whom. This programme will also provide an initial view of roles and responsibilities, although, as the next step, these will need to be defined to a fine level of detail, ensuring that every practical eventuality is covered. There will then follow a period of another few weeks while these roles and responsibilities are overlaid onto the existing workforce. It may be that additional personnel will need to be recruited or that some existing personnel will require additional training. This is to be expected, as we shall effectively be reconfiguring the workforce to match the requirement. This process shall, itself, take a few weeks until everything is nicely bedded in and working like a well-oiled machine.

DOI: 10.1201/9781003360674-15

Having got the right mix and profile of personnel in place, the next step is the discovery and listing of all existing certificates. This can be quite a job within a large organisation as it might well be found that there are a number of certificates which are serving no particular purpose. If these are self-signed certificates, they may simply be destroyed or reallocated if possible. If they are commercially bought certificates, then, depending upon their stated purpose, they may need to be revoked via the certificate authority concerned. This process will need to be undertaken for every single application and service which, together, constitute the IT estate. While, initially, this task will be undertaken by the development and support personnel, there may be several situations which require reference to the central PKI team in order to make the right decision. Consequently, this discovery process might take several weeks and, indeed, it may never actually cease as there will always be the odd stray certificate that no one really knows anything about. However, this task is fundamental to getting the PKI working as it should and should therefore be undertaken with enthusiasm and pride.

In parallel with the discovery phase, the central PKI team will be populating the certificate database, ensuring that they have full information as appertaining to every certificate being used within the organisation and, of course, those certificates from other organisations which may be required in order to encrypt data traversing the network and going onto other networks. This list of other, third-party certificates must also be held within the certificate database and kept up to date. Queries may be run against the database periodically in order to check such things. We must understand which of our own servers require which third-party certificates and why. We must also verify the contact details for third-party certificates and monitor them for expiration, just as we do for our own certificates. Similarly, we must understand which third-party organisations might hold our certificates and public keys. If we have not been managing the PKI in-house for a period of time, bringing all of this information up to date may appear, at first, as a daunting task. However, if a methodical approach is taken, it is a task which may be systematically worked on until, finally, it is complete. When this point is reached, we can sigh a sigh of relief as, from that point onwards, everything will be much more easily managed. Provided, of course, that the automated renewal messages have been configured properly for internally held certificates, those which are held by third parties and those third-party certificates held by our own organisation.

When all of these tasks have been completed, the central PKI team may embark upon the task of providing regular reports from the certificate database. The first task here is, of course, to specify exactly what those reports should be. Then, they need to be built and tested. Finally, the reports should be checked by those at director level in order to ensure that they represent a thorough view of what is happening within the PKI. This should be straightforward enough if the PKI team have understood the requirements from the organisation perspective. A set of reports produced at a given point in time also represent a snapshot view of the entire IT infrastructure and are thus valuable from several perspectives.

Unsurprisingly, the tasks mentioned above will have taken many weeks. Probably, a period of around three months or more would be required for a typical, medium-sized organisation, providing a good approach is followed. But it must all be actively managed. Things will not happen by magic. There will be a good deal of work required by all those involved if the end point of having an accurate view of the PKI estate is to be realised.

In addition to these basic tasks of defining the project approach, defining roles and responsibilities, recruiting the right personnel, getting everyone in place and aware of their immediate tasks, initiating the certificate discovery and listing process and generally getting things off the ground, the central PKI team must also build the organisational PKI infrastructure, according to a solid architectural approach. Different database types have already been discussed and, it is likely that, in many cases a Lightweight Directory Access Protocol (LDAP) directory server would meet the requirements. For this, one might embrace the OpenLDAP philosophy, as a solid offering which is available at no cost and well documented. Staying in the Open Source area, we could also use OpenSSL for the creation of certificates and something like EJBCA as a well-proven certificate authority. And, naturally, we would make use of the Online Certificate Status Protocol (OCSP) service in order to check other certificates against revocation lists. There are a few other little Open Source services and products which might be brought into the picture, but the main point here is that it will be possible to build a robust, scalable PKI infrastructure at absolutely no cost, using readily available, proven tools, for which the source code is readily available. Building things this way has several advantages. Firstly, the zero cost of all the tools you need. Compare this with the cost of buying in a commercial PKI product which, while being loaded with features, will still need installing, configuring and running for a while before it is doing anything useful. Furthermore, there will be an associated steep learning curve for your in-house personnel who will have to work just as hard, if not harder, to manage the organisation's PKI using such a tool, the cost of which will be perpetual, year on year. Secondly, by building things from the ground up using Open Source products, the personnel involved (the PKI team plus a few other developers) will become intimately familiar with how the system is constructed and how it is working. They will know it inside out and, if anything is not working optimally, they will quickly be able to rectify the issue. With a closed, commercial system, this simply is not possible. In addition, with a closed commercial system, it is not unusual for reported bug fixes to take several months before they are attended to. This is hardly ideal if the bug is causing problems for your organisation.

The in-house knowledge gained by building your own PKI infrastructure from the ground up is simply priceless. It enables the development of skills which will serve the organisation very well as it progresses. It also ensures that the system will be properly built, step by step, and will operate efficiently and optimally within the context of the organisation. It is the obvious way to go.

In terms of time scales, if we were starting from scratch with an inherited, chaotic collection of certificates and little in-house knowledge of them, it might take six months to bring it under a well-ordered control. However, this would represent an investment in time that would bring dividends to the organisation from many perspectives, providing the Open Source approach is taken. In terms of time scales, if a sophisticated commercial product is bought, installed and run, it will take just as long, if not longer, before the certificate estate is fully under control. However, this approach would not provide the aforementioned dividends to the organisation and would also involve a very significant initial and ongoing cost. This cost may be thought of as net profit, or operational budget, walking out of the door, month by month, with absolutely no return on investment to the organisation. And so, there is another way of looking at time scales. With the self-built, in-house approach, there would be an investment in personnel but no additional software costs and no ongoing running costs. With the bought-in commercial approach, there is the same investment in personnel, plus a very significant initial cost of the software, plus a very significant ongoing licence cost, plus a very significant ongoing support cost. These additional costs will be borne by the organisation for as long as they run the commercial system which, for some, will be for as long as they remain in operation. These significant costs are on top of the existing operating costs of the organisation concerned. When everything you need is freely available, well documented and you may have the source code of it yourself, it would seem to make little sense to go down the commercial route. If, within the organisation, one of the reasons given for using a commercial product is that the organisation does not need to worry about it, or understand how it works, or maintain it, such reasoning is heavily flawed. If the organisation does not know how the system is working, then it does not understand its own PKI and shall not be in a position to fix things if something breaks (which it will). Furthermore, it will still need to worry about it, and it will still need to maintain it. The supplier will, from time to time, issue updates to the system (which are usually just additional complications), and the organisation will be obliged to install them if they want to keep their system supported. The problem here is that such updates may or may not be compatible with the organisation's existing infrastructure. There may be dependencies which are taken for granted by the supplier but which may not be present within the organisation's IT. When this happens, and it frequently happens, things tend to break and the organisation is faced with yet more costs as the situation will be considered outside the bounds of the agreed support package from the supplier.

With the in-house approach, the time scales are fairly clear cut. The system needs to be designed, built and run. With the commercial approach, there really is no end to the time scales as the organisation will be constantly tinkering with the system and the operational staff will be constantly having to update their understanding of it in their efforts to support it. And so, the short answer to the question posed by this chapter is, it all depends on how you approach the issue. If one takes the sensible, in-house design build and maintain approach, probably around six months would see the organisation in a very strong position with a well-designed and well-understood PKI that will be easily supported. If one takes the alternative approach, the answer is that it will take as long as your organisation remains in place. Taking the ancient Egyptian metaphor again, the first approach produces order out of chaos in a relatively short space of time. The alternative approach will maintain a state of chaos until 'the end of days'.

SUMMARY

This chapter has taken a practical look at what it takes to actually implement a robust PKI. It has been stressed that there are tangible advantages to developing such a system in-house using freely available Open Source tools which have all been well proven. Furthermore, the organisation would be in possession of the source code and the skills developed throughout the project will ensure that the resulting system may easily be supported. It has additionally been shown that taking the alternative approach of simply buying in a commercial product is, actually, fraught with difficulties and saddles the organisation with a very significant additional cost which is ongoing for as long as the system or the organisation remains. The time scales, in real terms, are consequently heavily dependent upon which approach is taken. On the one hand, they can be planned, designed and executed and are therefore finite; on the other, they are ongoing, in all probability for the life of the organisation.

Chapter 16

What skills are required for operational personnel?

Understanding associated technologies

The in-house model which has been promoted in previous chapters is a good model. Furthermore, it is a straightforward model for which the required skills are fairly clear cut. In addition, when putting together the core public key infrastructure (PKI) team, these will be easy skills to demonstrate at the time of interview, and so, the organisation may have a reasonable confidence as to the capabilities of those being recruited. Obviously, the starting point is a good understanding of IT in general. Note, that this does not mean just an understanding of software. Prospective employees should understand how computers actually work. How a mainframe is constructed differently from a traditional server. The difference between the latter and a server card within a 19″ rack. What i.p. addresses are, how network cards work, what load balancers are, why a hardware-based firewall is desirable, how network-attached storage works, how mainframe storage is partitioned and so on. If they can demonstrate a confident knowledge of such items, then they will likely be quite sound. In addition, they should understand the differences between operating systems, file systems and how encryption works, the principles behind a relational database and so on. They should certainly have a working knowledge of Linux. This may seem like a tall order, but there are thousands of good people who have been made redundant or otherwise pushed out in favour of outsourcing and so there are plenty of skills around at the moment. The organisation should not be shy of recruiting senior individuals either, as these people bring with them a wealth of experience and knowledge that may be passed down within the organisation. Indeed, succession planning should be high on the human resources (HR) agenda.

The individuals being interviewed for the core PKI team also need to have a working understanding of open-source software, what it is, why it works as it does, how it is supported and so on. If they are familiar with Linux and how to configure and install it from the command line, then they have a head start. And, if they are familiar with Linux, then a good question to ask them is which Linux distribution do they favour and why? Then, we need to

DOI: 10.1201/9781003360674-16

get on to the skills they will need for the various approaches that may be taken to getting a PKI running smoothly. They should be able to demonstrate a knowledge of OpenSSL, OpenLDAP and EJBCA plus other components and services that may be used in the construction of a working PKI. Such skills are mostly based upon the idea of configuring services via scripts, using the language of the chosen service itself.

If we look at OpenLDAP as an example, and assuming a typical Linux server, it is not too difficult for an individual with proven skills to establish the directory server. Having downloaded and unpacked the software, it starts with establishing a configuration script, with this simple command:

```
./configure
```

The software may then be 'built' after establishing the necessary dependencies. This is done like this:

```
make dependmake
```

In addition, a simple test suite in order to test that the build has been successful may be established with the simple command:

```
make test
```

After which, assuming that you have 'super user' privileges, which you should have if you are building something like this, the software may be formally installed with the command:

```
su root -c 'make install'
```

As may be seen, this is all quite intuitive, and an experienced Linux professional will have no difficulty at all with it and the software will be installed, typically under the /usr/local directory structure. Now, it will be necessary to edit the configuration file which is named slapd.ldif and provided as part of the package, to include the provision of the database component. Something like this:

```
dn: olcDatabase=mdb,cn=config
objectClass: olcDatabaseConfig
objectClass: olcMdbConfig
olcDatabase: mdb
OlcDbMaxSize: 1073741824
olcSuffix: dc=<OUR-ORGANISATION-DOMAIN>,dc=<COM>
olcRootDN: cn=Manager,dc=<OUR-ORGANISATION-DOMAIN>,dc=<COM>
olcRootPW: secret
olcDbDirectory: /usr/local/var/openldap-data
olcDbIndex: objectClass eq
```

Now, we can import the configuration database with the command:

```
su root -c /usr/local/sbin/slapadd -n 0 -F /usr/local/etc/
slapd.d -l /usr/local/etc/openldap/slapd.ldif
```

Now, we can start the LDAP Daemon with another simple command:

```
su root -c /usr/local/libexec/slapd -F /usr/local/etc/
slapd.d
```

All of this is very well documented within various free on-line resources, with manuals that may be downloaded and with plenty of example scripts and so, as may be seen, it is really not that difficult or time consuming. In order to add entries to our directory, we shall need to use the 'ldapadd' command, once we have created an LDAP Data Interchange Format (LDIF) file with which to place some structure on the entries. This we can do like this:

```
dn: dc=<OUR-ORGANISATION-DOMAIN>,dc=<COM>
objectclass: dcObject
objectclass: organisation
o: <OUR ORGANISATION>
dc: <OUR-ORGANISATION-DOMAIN>
dn: cn=Manager,dc=<OUR-ORGANISATION-DOMAIN>,dc=<COM>
objectclass: organisationalRole
cn: Manager
```

Now, we may add entries into our new directory with the command:

```
ldapadd -x -D "cn=Manager,dc=<OUR-ORGANISATION-
DOMAIN>,dc=<COM>" -W -f example.ldif
```

And it is all, more or less, as simple as that. There are additional commands and customisations that may be used, according to the design specification arrived at by the core PKI team, but the above example provides a 'bare bones' set of instructions which, as may be noted, are all quite intuitive. This is the beauty of using open-source products in order to build the PKI infrastructure. An experienced Linux developer will be able to do everything and, furthermore, will have all of the source code readily available, should anything need to be modified. In addition, the scripts written to build and run these components are effectively self-documenting. This means that, should a developer leave or move to a different department within the organisation, another developer can look at the scripts and understand exactly what is going on. These skills are not difficult to find at the moment, but they need to be brought in-house and nurtured. Otherwise, they may effectively disappear, forcing the organisation to buy in products and/or outsource the IT function.

In order to create certificates, the same sort of skills may be applied to OpenSSL, which, typically will already be installed as an integral component of many Linux distributions, often found under the /etc/ssl directory structure with related certificates stored under /etc/ssl/certs; however, these locations may vary from distribution to distribution and you may, for various reasons, decide to establish an alias that points towards these paths. If an older version of OpenSSL is installed or, for some other reason, one wishes to build the service from scratch, then there is, as expected, a configuration file which may be used for that purpose, prior to build. It will look something like this:

```
$ ./config \
--prefix=/opt/openssl \
--openssldir=/opt/openssl \
no-shared \
-DOPENSSL_TLS_SECURITY_LEVEL=2 \
enable-ec_nistp_64_gcc_128
```

Then, we may prepare to compile the code, by first establishing the dependencies:

```
$ make depend
```

Then, running the compile to build the main package:

```
$ make
$ make test
$ sudo make install
```

Something like the following will appear in /opt/openssl:

```
drwxr-xr-x 2 root root  4096 Jun 3 08:49 bin
drwxr-xr-x 2 root root  4096 Jun 3 08:49 certs
drwxr-xr-x 3 root root  4096 Jun 3 08:49 include
drwxr-xr-x 4 root root  4096 Jun 3 08:49 lib
drwxr-xr-x 6 root root  4096 Jun 3 08:48 man
drwxr-xr-x 2 root root  4096 Jun 3 08:49 misc
-rw-r--r-- 1 root root 10835 Jun 3 08:49 openssl.cnf
drwxr-xr-x 2 root root  4096 Jun 3 08:49 private
```

And then, eventually, we can make sure that existing certificates end up in the right certificate stores and that we can create new ones using the plethora of tools and options that make up OpenSSL. To get an idea of the scope of these, the $ openssl help command may be run, which will return a listing of the various utilities and functions available. Any of these may be expanded upon by typing 'man' followed by the command in order to examine the comprehensive manual pages. The list might look something like this:

Standard commands

```
asn1parse       ca      ciphers    cms     crl     crl2pkcs7
dgst     dhparam    dsa              dsaparam    ec
ecparam     enc       engine        errstr      gendsa
genpkey     genrsa         help      list
nseq      ocsp     passwd      pkcs12     pkcs7      pkcs8
pkey     pkeyparam     pkeyutl            prime      rand
rehash     req      rsa        rsautl      s _
client     s _ server     s _ time           sess _ id
smime      speed     spkac      srp       storeutl       ts
verify      version          x509
```

Message Digest commands (see the `dgst' command for more details)

```
blake2b512       blake2s256        gost       md4       md5
rmd160       sha1          sha224      sha256
sha3-224      sha3-256      sha3-384     sha3-512
sha384        sha512      sha512-224     sha512-256
shake128      shake256      sm3
```

Cipher commands (see the `enc' command for more details)

```
aes-128-cbc       aes-128-ecb        aes-192-cbc       aes-192-
ecb      aes-256-cbc      aes-256-ecb       aria-128-cbc
aria-128-cfb      aria-128-cfb1      aria-128-cfb8     aria-
128-ctr      aria-128-ecb      aria-128-ofb       aria-192-cbc
aria-192-cfb      aria-192-cfb1
aria-192-cfb8      aria-192-ctr      aria-192-ecb      aria-
192-ofb      aria-256-cbc      aria-256-cfb      aria-256-
cfb1      aria-256-cfb8      aria-256-ctr       aria-256-ecb
aria-256-ofb      base64       bf          bf-cbc
bf-cfb       bf-ecb       bf-ofb         camellia-
128-cbc      camellia-128-ecb    camellia-192-cbc    camellia-192-ecb
camellia-256-cbc
camellia-256-ecb    cast       cast-cbc        cast5-cbc
cast5-cfb       cast5-ecb
cast5-ofb       des        des-cbc        des-
cfb      des-ecb       des-ede       des-ede-cbc
des-ede-cfb      des-ede-ofb      des-ede3        des-ede3-
cbc      des-ede3-cfb
des-ede3-ofb      des-ofb       des3        desx
rc2       rc2-40-cbc       rc2-64-cbc       rc2-cbc
rc2-cfb       rc2-ecb       rc2-ofb        rc4
rc4-40       seed        seed-cbc        seed-
cfb      seed-ecb       seed-ofb        sm4-cbc
sm4-cfb
sm4-ctr       sm4-ecb        sm4-ofb
```

As one may readily appreciate, this represents quite a list of options. Compare this with what help you would get within a closed, commercial system and you may appreciate why many turn towards open-source tools. It may also be beneficial to check the existing trust stores on the system and, if necessary, create a new one from scratch. There is a good deal more we could cover but, suffice it to say, you will not be short of options with OpenSSL. When we are ready to create new keys and certificates, the code is fairly straightforward and any developer or PKI core team member who has got this far will have absolutely no difficulty in this respect.

Setting up your own certificate authority using EJBCA is equally straightforward, especially if the developer or PKI team member has a knowledge of JAVA. There are some JAVA-based dependencies to take into consideration. These include, OpenJDK which is the primary JAVA build environment, plus JBoss, which is an application hosting environment, a database tool such as MySQL or PostgreSQL and Apache Ant which is a build tool for JAVA. With these utilities in place, one may proceed to yet another configuration file, which includes sections for default properties, cesecore properties, ejbca properties, web properties, database properties and database protection properties. The entries in each of these sections are straightforward, and there is a wealth of documentation available with which to steer the developer through the process. Then, we can move forward to building the database, and good information is available for a variety of databases. We then configure the application server before, finally, building and deploying the EJBCA.

It may be seen from the above comments and examples that building an organisational PKI from the ground up is not that difficult a task if the open-source route is taken. Those with basic development skills in Linux/UNIX, JAVA and one or more of the popular scripting languages such as Perl, Python, PHP, plus use of the BASH shell scripts, will have absolutely no difficulty. Consequently, when looking for a skill set among prospective employees, or within the existing complement, it will not be difficult to establish who is likely to be helpful either as a member of the core PKI team, or as an associated developer or support person whose PKI-related skills may be enhanced.

Alternatively, if the bought-in product route is taken, then a slightly different set of skills will be required. The only skills that you will be able to measure prior to the event will be a knowledge of the organisational infrastructure and the ability to install complex software according to a client–server model. Obviously, such personnel will also need a working understanding of PKI, both conceptually and actually. After buying the said software, then the fun will really start as it will quickly become evident that each vendor does things their own way and that your operational personnel will have a very steep learning curve as they have to learn, from the ground up, a very complex and often sprawling application that may not appear to work logically. The staff will not know what to do when the software fails to find all the certificates and they will probably end up entering everything, one certificate at a time, having to check things like i.p. addresses, purposes and, of course, enter in the expiry dates. Getting to know such a piece of software will be a time-consuming exercise. If there are integral help files at all, they will probably be quite sparse and will no doubt just keep referring the user to the vendor's web site where finding what they want will vary from being tedious to impossible. Indeed, looking through the web sites of the primary vendors, there is a great deal of talk about 'solutions' or offering 'PKI as a service' or integration with your 'DevOps' culture, and there are a few actual products mentioned, but no screen shots, no installation instructions, no operation instructions. So, how is one to choose between them when they are saying roughly the same thing – which is absolutely nothing. There are endless blindingly obvious explanations of PKI, coupled to so-called 'case studies' which tell you nothing about the product. In fact, it is impossible to discover how the product works or even what it looks like, let alone what dependencies it might have. And, of course, there is absolutely no mention at all of cost. To discover what it might cost, you would have to engage with the company concerned, whose initial gambit will be "well, it all depends". Then, they will try their level best to set up a meeting with you on your premises, in order that they might find out more about your organisation, how it works and who the key people are, especially those making purchasing decisions. One might take a philosophical view and say that this is to be expected these days. Maybe it is, but it will not help you make sensible purchasing decisions if you think that this is the way forward for your organisation. If you speak to three or four such vendors, all that will happen is that it will end up being a 'Dutch auction' and you will likely choose the least expensive option, while still having absolutely no idea of how the product works and, importantly, how it might work on your infrastructure. This is a far cry from the well-documented and easy-to-understand open-source route. However, if an organisation did decide to purchase a ready-made product, then it would make sense to try it on approval for three months in order to better understand it. This is reasonable, except, if you are doing this for five products, it will be a hugely time-consuming and confusing undertaking, within which you will find many contradictory ideas and approaches to the same underlying requirement.

Then, there is the microservices and DevOps approach where, in fact, you will need all the components articulated in the open-source discussion only now, you will further complicate the picture with the use of containers, runtime layers and service meshes which will require a completely different and additional skill set. First of all, you will need to decide which components will be represented by which containers and where these containers will be situated. So, you will require an additional architecture which shall need to be carefully considered, designed and communicated before you do anything. And this architecture should explicitly describe the PKI and how it is going to work. The concept of containers is not really new. As mentioned in earlier chapters, you could already achieve the same effect with Delphi packages or you could even call simple DLLs (dynamic link libraries) from multiple applications. The idea is that the container is a package which contains everything necessary to run the service or application that it represents. So, if you have multiple containers, representing multiple applications, sitting on a particular server, each container will utilise the operating system resources which reside on that server. They will each require access to the kernel, to the processor and to system memory, just as individually compiled applications would have done. In fact, more resources are required to run the container model as there is a good deal of duplication going on, as each container is including similar elements of the operating system, plus an additional container management layer is required. The end result is the same: several applications which are pertinent to your organisation run on an infrastructure which consists of hardware servers and data storage. However, the container model has sparked something of a revolution in the development world and, no doubt, many fortunes will be made from it as a result. Similarly, many traditional IT infrastructures will be destroyed by it.

In order to have a container, you have to have somewhere to put it. You could build it on your own infrastructure, but you will find no mention of this among the container and DevOps evangelists and the endless conferences that have sprung up. No, they all insist that everything is placed in the cloud. Doing so means that, effectively, you are giving away all of your priceless organisational data, intellectual property and IT into somebody else's hands. Your organisation-specific information, including your financial transactions, your employee data, your customer data and so on, will be sitting on somebody's hardware infrastructure, somewhere, but you have no idea where. It could be anywhere in the world, from Indonesia to Mexico, India, absolutely anywhere, wherever the cloud supplier company finds it cheapest to deploy. Furthermore, this hardware infrastructure will be administered and supported by somebody, but who? You have absolutely no idea. But that person may well have access to all of your organisation's sensitive data. No wonder we keep hearing about data breaches and the loss of information. If you ask any passing five-year old, does it make sense to give all of your knowledge and private information away to an unknown third party? They will probably quickly answer, "no it doesn't". And yet, this is precisely what government agencies and commercial enterprises are doing everyday. Why do they do it? Because someone has told them that it saves money and that, furthermore, they won't have to worry about maintaining their own infrastructure or keep on the support staff. But if you already have your own infrastructure, which has been paid for, and everything is nicely under your own control, why would you pay for it all over again in order to place it somewhere where you have no control over it? In addition, every organisation who has gone down this route has suffered significant additional IT costs. However, there it is. The Emperor's new clothes are fitting nicely.

So, first of all, it is necessary to buy a cloud service from a cloud supplier, who will charge according to their particular whim. The cost will bear little relation to what it actually costs them, because they have the necessary economies of scale. Having purchased some space via the cloud supplier, which, by the way, you will be paying for for ever more, containers may now be placed on servers within *their* infrastructure. However, to get them there is not that straightforward. A container 'image' is required, from which you use a manifest file (written in yet another scripting language named YAML, which is actually quite intuitive) in order to build your container runtime, which is the code block which will sit on the server space allocated to your organisation within the cloud. But another component is needed in order to manage your containers, and that component also sits in your cloud space. There are variations on the theme, but one of the most popular management components is Docker. Docker allows developers to develop and deploy their containers in a fairly straightforward manner, providing that the Docker engine is present on the server that hosts your containers. Oh, and by the way, your container images must be listed in a repository in order that the manifest may find them and thus build the containers, which then need to be deployed. If this all sounds a little complicated, compared with just building your application and putting it on one of your servers, that's because it is. It is hugely more complicated and will soak up a huge amount of development time and effort. Furthermore, the end result will soak up huge amounts of processing and associated cost. However, if the idea is appealing to your organisation, then there are plenty of bolt-on services available.

One of the issues with containers is that they tend to grow in number almost exponentially. Of course, because developers may now spend time writing endless numbers of application ideas, whether they are required or not, and deploying them, using a third-party service, onto a third-party infrastructure. Consequently, the organisation finds itself having to increase its provision of 'cloud' space, at the appropriate cost, and the whole mess of hundreds of containers slowly becomes unmanageable. But that's OK, because the organisation may then spend some more money on something called a 'service mesh' which will look at all the containers how they are supposed to be communicating with each other and will attempt to automate the process. So, now the organisation has even less control over its IT estate. And who is documenting all of this? Who has drawn up a plan of every microservice and every container, showing exactly where it is deployed and what it communicates with? And where is the ongoing plan? Being able to throw up three or four builds of a container in one day is not clever, as is often claimed. It is, in fact, rather unintelligent as it is impossible to maintain a suitable test rigour under such circumstances. And if, in addition, nothing is really documented or planned, then a fairly significant risk is being taken within such an application development model. This fact should be taken into consideration.

What does this mean in terms of skills? Well, it means that in addition to all the skills mentioned in the first part of this chapter, developers and the core PKI team will now have to learn how to create container images, place them in a repository, write manifest files in YAML and use an overall container management system such as Docker. Does that mean that the organisation will be able to create applications which it previously could not? No, it doesn't. Does it mean that the organisation will be able to create applications more efficiently? No, it doesn't. Does it mean that the organisation will have a better grasp of its PKI estate? No, it doesn't. Does it mean that the organisation will be able to manage it's PKI any better? No, it doesn't. What it does mean is a lot more cost and complexity and the requirement of another skill set among the developers and support staff involved. Of course, under the DevOps model, there will hardly be any support staff as developers will simply keep putting up new builds daily, or multiple times within a day. Does this mean that your applications do not require support? No, it doesn't. Of course, all of this is obscured under the 'cloud native applications' model which assumes that everything has to be in the cloud. There is even a Cloud Native Computing Foundation which has members across the world and seems to believe that there is safety in numbers. The more people admiring the Emperor's new clothes, the more they must be real. It is a foundation of developers who pretend that they are end user driven. You will be hard pushed to find an end user who has ever heard of them. The end user is the consumer of the services that your organisation provides. Not the developers within your organisation. That is simply a self-serving model whose only achievement is to complicate things beyond measure. I am again reminded of the ancient Egyptian prediction of chaos preceding the 'end of days'. Someone within the organisation needs to be keeping the end of days at arm's length.

So, what does the container model mean for PKI? It means that the organisation will suddenly multiply the number of certificates that it needs to manage in leaps and bounds. If it was previously managing a few hundred, now it will be managing a few thousand, or tens of thousands or, in some cases, hundreds of thousands. Does that make the organisation or its transactions any more secure? No, it doesn't. Does it mean easier management of certificates and keys? No, it doesn't. But it will certainly involve an increase in cost and, when something goes wrong, it will really go wrong. By now, the reader may understandably be wondering how on earth are certificates managed at all in this container model. The answer is with great difficulty. If you have at least some of your infrastructure in-house, you may manage the PKI for that easily enough. If some of it is in the cloud and residing within virtual machines which remain static, then they are not too difficult to manage. But containers may be built and destroyed within the same day. And each time, any certificates upon which they relied will need to be renewed. Within a service mesh (such as the popular Istio for example), there is typically an integral certificate authority (CA) in order to provision certificates quickly which, in turn, allow for microservices and containers to communicate using Transport Layer Security (TLS)/Secure Sockets Layer (SSL) protocols. One issue with these integral CAs built into service meshes is that they are almost invisible from a security and compliance perspective. Also, they do not easily integrate with external CAs which means that developers will be effectively issuing thousands of self-signed certificates which have little value from a security perspective.

The service mesh allows for the management of communications between microservices and containers, as well as implementing load balancing. This latter feature, while sounding impressive, may be disastrous from a PKI perspective. If containers are moved around randomly according to perceived load balancing requirements, then their certificates and associated connections must follow. Which means the issuance of yet more relatively untrusted, self-signed certificates. In any event, it should not be necessary to load balance if the organisational IT architecture has been well designed. But of course, in cloud native land, the architecture and associated infrastructure no longer belongs to the organisation. So, whose load are you balancing? A good question. Nevertheless, the service mesh will automatically be doing this. Now, the organisation will require a number of externally supplied certificates from trusted third-party CAs, certainly for all of its externally facing applications. The service mesh may be able to do this, but who is going to instruct it to do so and, in any event, how is the PKI core team, who are also concerned with security, going to be able to control this? The answer is that they cannot. There exists a fundamental dichotomy between the DevOps philosophy of unnecessarily fast build and deployment and the cyber security philosophy of enforcing policies and control over the way things are built and run and, especially, over the issuance of certificates. How can this be resolved? By adding yet another layer. This time another control layer which integrates with the service mesh but allows certificates to be sourced from either the service mesh CA, the enterprise-level CA (approved by security) and external CAs (also approved by security). That sounds fine, but it represents yet another fairly significant cost and more complexity as such tools usually simply piggy back on the service mesh which will, naturally, impact the performance of the service mesh. Of course, you will be able to issue thousands more certificates, and the additional layer will typically provide you with a window in which you can see them all listed. But what good is that to you in practice? You will need to become adept at searching for rogue certificates.

As might be imagined, the skill set required to understand and grapple with all of this is complex and, what is more, it is a skill set which is entirely additional to what you already had. So, you will either require a lot more developers who have this skill set or you will expect to burden your existing staff with learning all of these new technologies and associated tricks. It is notable that none of this enables the organisation to do anything that they were not already doing. But it complicates the organisational PKI like the devil.

SUMMARY

In this chapter, the skill sets required for different models of deployment have been discussed and evaluated. It has been shown that the development and infrastructure model chosen by the organisation has a very significant effect upon the skills required in order to maintain a PKI. If using an in-house infrastructure, then, with the use of a few open-source tools, things may be kept relatively simple and manageable. If an external, cloud-based infrastructure is used, the PKI quickly becomes unmanageable and the skill set required in order to understand why is significantly different from that of the simple, in-house model. If third-party, commercial-closed source tools are bought in, the organisation will quickly lose control of its PKI anyway, especially if using a cloud-based infrastructure. It has been demonstrated that the cloud native 'Emperor's new clothes' syndrome spells disaster for PKI and that the organisation will be forced to add layer upon layer of technology in order to exert any meaningful management over it. This can never be a good thing. If an organisation goes down this road, it may expect to spend a lot of time talking about and playing with technology, instead of focusing upon its core function. Furthermore, it will spend a good deal of money in the process.

Chapter 17

How do we embed a PKI culture in the workplace?

Communication

Public key infrastructure (PKI) is unlike most elements of IT that end users are exposed to. They usually work with completed applications and don't really care what is happening behind the scenes, as long as everything works as expected and is reliable. Typically, they will have some small understanding of traditional networks, but none at all of the cloud and how things work there, or the implications of moving data onto a third-party infrastructure. That PKI underpins all of these things will be beyond the compass of their understanding. Consequently, it is clear that, in most cases, some sort of communications activity will be necessary for the general, non-IT literate staff within the organisation. That is one activity. Another is a communications activity to the IT personnel, some of whom will have some sort of understanding, at least at a theoretical level, while others may have heard the term but will really know nothing at all about it. The PKI core team must therefore have this two-pronged communication plan fairly high on their agenda and should be implementing it systematically right from the start. Furthermore, it is not something to be undertaken once and then forgotten. They must keep everyone informed and up to date with what is going on, why and how things are progressing. In short, they must embed a PKI-aware culture across the organisation. In most cases, this will be no mean feat and shall require a good deal of precise planning and organisation. This also presupposes that a decision has been made to actively manage the PKI internally.

The first step will be to identify logical groups of personnel within the organisation. For example, directors and senior managers, executive middle management, administration including finance, IT personnel and everybody else. That would provide five such groups for which tailored presentations with supporting materials may be configured. There may be more, depending upon the structure of your organisation. These supporting materials might include simple schematic diagrams to describe the theory, general informational documents and detailed code examples, depending upon the group in question. The challenge will be to get the message across that each group *needs* to understand and then to ensure that they have understood it.

DOI: 10.1201/9781003360674-17

Then, when someone mentions an errant certificate or a communication handshake that has broken, people will understand what they are talking about. Even more important, among end users, they will develop the ability to spot possible PKI-related problems and report them back to the PKI core team. In a way, this may be seen as an expansion of the core team which embraces the entire organisation. Yes, everyone should be aware of the importance of the PKI to the continued smooth running of the organisation.

We might usefully consider these identified groups (which may be slightly different in your organisation) and think about what they need to understand about the organisational PKI. We may then tailor our various materials and presentations accordingly.

Directors and senior managers would traditionally have little enough interest in IT in general, let alone PKI. Their primary consideration to date will have been simply one of cost. This maybe rather unintelligent, but it is the only measure they know how to apply. This is why they are so easily persuaded by the 'lobbyists' and 'consultants' from the giant IT organisations. They simply believe what they are told, because they don't know any better and, unfortunately, they rarely listen to what their own staff are telling them. So, they are an audience used to being wined, dined and coerced by clever individuals from the big IT companies, and the core PKI team has to somehow compete with this reality, but how? Well, shock is a good tactic. Explaining to them that you have something to reveal to them which might have dire consequences for the organisation, whether it be a government ministry, a commercial enterprise or an academic institution. The task is then to get them to agree to come together for a meeting where all shall be revealed. At such a meeting, the importance of PKI to the organisation may be stressed and, depending upon what development model is being followed, the importance of managing it all in-house and, if need be, bringing things back to your own infrastructure may be covered. Leaving them in no doubt as to what can happen when the PKI fails, and what this means to the organisation, should help to make them sympathetic towards the internal PKI project. Explaining things properly will also give them a working knowledge of PKI, and so, they will be more likely to agree to whatever is needed in order to proceed properly. The importance of getting this group on board cannot be stressed too highly. If they do not believe in the PKI project, then they will not properly support it and things will be difficult for the core PKI team and everyone else involved, right from the start. In order to obtain their support, they must first understand what it is all about and how important it is. They may be left with a short paper which explains such matters succinctly and clearly.

The executive middle management group can be difficult. They believe that they are the ones who make all the decisions and are therefore the most important. They have a tendency to believe that they know everything. In fact, their understanding is often fairly shallow and they simply repeat what has been fed to them by external consultants. Some of them will be good and will have a good understanding of how the organisation really works, although this understanding may not be complete in its coverage. Getting their support and understanding will be difficult as they will undoubtedly consider the PKI folk as simply part of a resource that works for them. The way to approach them may be to explain to them that a great opportunity exists here, with which to consolidate and, in some cases, transform the organisation that they are responsible for. They may be given a good degree of technical explanation. They may not understand it all properly, but they will understand that it is something important and that, perhaps, they should have an involvement in it. They may be invited to do so in several areas, such as recruitment and the decision to build and maintain everything in-house. If two or three of these individuals can be brought on side, then they will be of great value to the project overall. They might also, slowly, bring the other members of their group with them, as the realisation that this is important takes hold. It will be vitally important to keep this group informed at all times and, when their support is required, it must be requested outright and without hesitation. Make them feel involved and important and they will support the PKI initiative. Furthermore, their support may prove invaluable at several points as the project path is followed.

The administration and finance group may be considered as the primary end users. They will be the ones most affected if and when something goes wrong. Depending upon the recent history of IT development within the organisation, they may have a healthy degree of scepticism about anything that someone from the IT department tells them. This is actually a good quality and one which may be played upon in order to win their support. The fundamental workings of PKI may be explained to them and scenarios covered wherein it is possible for things to go wrong and affect the applications that they are working with. This may be especially pertinent to the finance group. It may be explained to them that every transaction they undertake depends absolutely upon the PKI. The overall project may be explained to them and they, more than any other group, should be invited to ask questions and to give their own experiences of IT-related problems, because *all* of these problems will be down to errors in coding at the application level or with the correct management of certificates. The core PKI team may therefore sympathise with whatever is revealed to them by this group and, as far as they can, explain why they have had the problems which they have experienced. The project may also be explained to them at a high level, including the time scales involved and who will be doing what. They may be invited to inform the core PKI team of any communication-related errors between the applications that they are using. Ongoing communication with this group will be important as it is they who will discover the errors which slip by the IT department and, importantly, what these errors mean from an operational perspective.

The IT personnel group may prove to be a mixed bag. Undoubtedly, there will be some who will dig in their heels and see no reason to change their habits with respect to certificate management and the organisational PKI. Others will have their heads full of new technologies and radical approaches to things, especially if they have been attending conferences. And some may be solid, resilient types who understand the organisation and how it works, and who will listen to anything that affects its smooth running, especially if it is communications related. A good first step would be to obtain agreement within the group as to how applications are designed, built and deployed and, very importantly, why. Who was it that asked for them? Does their deployment really make any sense? Are there applications which might usefully be decommissioned? Such questions should trigger useful conversation which, in turn, may lead to a more coherent understanding of how all of this is working and why getting a grip on the PKI is so important, especially so if the cloud is being used for anything. This group may also be invited to formally submit their suggestions to the core PKI team in this context. There will be some good ideas surfacing here and they should all be carefully considered. As an integral part of this communication strand, the core PKI team may identify those individuals, from different application development areas, who are going to prove the most useful to the project overall. Those who have a deep knowledge of existing applications for example and those who are involved in the support of major databases and other important building blocks within the broader IT estate. Full technical details of how the core PKI group intends to establish a renewed and efficient PKI may be revealed to this group and any ensuing discussion will be most helpful in establishing the correctness of this approach.

The 'everyone else' group is really just anyone not covered by the abovementioned groups but who might have access to applications, however infrequently. It might also include anyone who just happens to take an interest in what is being said about the PKI. Such individuals should not be underestimated, they may not be directly involved but they may have latent knowledge and a good understanding of how the organisation actually works, right down to the lowest levels of granularity. Such knowledge is priceless, and if any such individual should appear, they should be welcomed and cosseted by the core PKI team. They will prove to be good allies and advocates for the project overall. In addition, they may be given full technical information as, undoubtedly, there will be some within this group who understand it all perfectly.

Working through such a communications programme might seem arduous at first, but it will quickly become apparent that it is a crucially important exercise. Furthermore, it will be very revealing and the core PKI team will be constantly discovering small, but important details of which they were not previously aware. This knowledge will all help to reinforce the project plan and ensure that what is being planned for the PKI is, in fact, the best possible solution for the organisation. It will also be a revealing exercise in discovering who your friends are. This aspect should not be underestimated. The PKI team should cultivate the positive relationships which ensue from this exercise as they will all become very important as the project progresses.

At the end of this exercise, or at least the first iteration of this exercise, for it shall need to be repeated often, the core PKI team will have a much better understanding of the organisation and how it operates. This understanding may be overlaid upon their original plan and, if need be, that plan may be adjusted with the hindsight of this additional knowledge. It is important that any such important project steps be immediately fed back into these groups, while thanking them for their continued support and participation. It will quickly become apparent to the core PKI team that this sort of internal communication is absolutely essential. The right people must be kept fully aware of what is going on at all times, for better or for worse. If this internal communication is neglected, the team concerned will be working in the dark and, eventually, will come up against major problems which could have been avoided. Yes, a PKI culture must certainly be well and truly embedded within the organisation and this should be considered a priority.

SUMMARY

This chapter has stressed the importance of internal communication to any project which aims to build or otherwise transform the organisational PKI. Suggestions have been made as to how to go about such an internal communications plan and how it might work in practice. A given organisation might vary the detail of this suggested plan but, in principle, it represents a sound approach as to how to let the organisation know what is going on while stressing the importance of the PKI. Observations have been made as to the likely response to such an exercise and how to manage such a response. It has been noted that individual character and associated knowledge play a large part here and that the communication plan must take such factors into consideration. In any event, a proper communications plan and ensuing activity should be seen as a core component of properly managing a PKI.

Chapter 18

How do we keep it working as we grow?

Planning and documentation

As has been shown, building a proper public key infrastructure (PKI) from scratch, or repairing one which is in a sorry state, is not a task for the faint-hearted. It requires understanding, planning and very careful execution. If properly undertaken, it will also have been very well documented and that is a factor which will pay dividends if, for various reasons, the PKI undergoes a significant increase in scale. The primary reasons for such an expansion in size may be as follows:

1. A natural growth in parallel with the expansion of the organisation as a whole. This might occur in parallel with a step change in the scale of operations undertaken by the organisation in question.
2. A sudden, dramatic increase in scale due to acquisitions, such as a commercial organisation buying a competitor or another company with a synergistic product offering. Or, perhaps the merging of two or more government agencies, or the reorganisation of departments which brings additional responsibilities to the host.
3. The decision to embrace the DevOps philosophy and the cloud by senior management, without fully realising the implications of doing so.

Either of the situations described above could mean a significant growth in both the number of certificates being managed and the sheer architectural scale of the PKI. There may be other scenarios which would have a similar impact. The primary point being that the PKI is unlikely to remain static. There are scenarios wherein it might actually decrease in scale, at least for a while, but mostly, it will increase, either gradually and in a well-ordered manner or dramatically due to a sudden acquisition or a move away from traditional development models to the DevOps model. The response from the core PKI team has to suit the occasion and, if the original PKI has been designed and executed properly, they will be able to meet the challenge without too much difficulty. The three scenarios depicted above shall now be explored in a little more detail.

When building or rebuilding a PKI, attention should be paid to documentation. Both architectural configuration and operational policies should all be described in detail and lodged somewhere safe. These are working documents which should be referred to regularly to ensure compliance and kept up to date with additions and revisions as appropriate. This being the case, the PKI may evolve and grow naturally, because it will do so according to clearly laid down policies and rules. If another server is added or a system is decommissioned, this will all be undertaken in an orderly manner, according to defined policies, and the documentation shall, as and where appropriate, be kept up to date. Within this operational framework, it shall be easy to determine if the PKI is becoming unwieldy, or if things have slipped and adjustment is necessary. It should never reach the point where certificates are expiring because they were not understood properly. Everything will be understood properly if associated work has been undertaken properly and in an ordered, systematic manner. And so, within this scenario, maintaining the PKI shall not become problematic because everything will be documented and under control. The same applies to personnel. If one or two additional people are required, then this requirement will have been foreseen and steps taken to ensure the smooth ongoing maintenance of everything. This is simply how things should be within a well-run organisation.

The second scenario, which will usually come about due to acquisitions and mergers, is a little more complicated. If two, or more, operational units are brought together and they each are running a PKI of some description, which will be the case, then a decision must be made as to which one of them is going to take precedence. Bear in mind, that each of them may have been constructed according to a different set of rules and each of them will have different policies in place. Making this decision will not be easy, especially if all seem to be operating in a reasonable manner. This is where the value of having a core PKI team comes to the fore. The core team may immediately undertake a project in order to examine and evaluate the various rules, policies and architectural configurations which exist in each case. Factors such as the location of certificate stores on servers running different operating systems, naming conventions, the processes and procedures for issuing and revoking certificates, the precise format of the organisational x.509 certificates and so on. As an output from this project, which should not take more than a couple of weeks, a decision will be made to standardise according to one of the models in place. This will probably be that of the host organisation, unless a better model is clearly discernible among one of the others. Having made the decision, then a clearly structured plan must be drawn up for migration, showing exactly how the other PKIs shall be brought in line with the host system. This will be an iterative operation, probably starting with the issuance process for new certificates, together with their precise specification. The location of certificate stores will, at first, be a little messy if different conventions have been followed.

The problem with changing or renaming the location of the certificate store on a given server is that everything referencing these certificates needs to know that the location has changed. In some cases, this might be a large number of entities. However, this task may be partly automated with some judicious script writing by knowledgeable personnel, and so, it is not an impossible one. It is a task which is worth the effort though. If there is just one other PKI, this will soon be undertaken. Then, the various policies, their definitions and meanings, must all be examined and brought into line. The simple way of achieving this, if the incoming PKI is divergent, is simply to replace all of their policies with that of the host. The larger part of this task is to make any personnel within the incoming organisation aware of the changes. But then, as part of the core PKI team's project plan, there will be a thorough communications exercise to the relevant staff of the incoming organisation, including their executive managers and directors (there will obviously be an attendant project to rationalise this personnel structure in any case, so the PKI team can piggy back onto this). In short, managing a sudden growth due to mergers and acquisitions will not be easy. However, if the task is undertaken methodically by the core PKI team within the host organisation, then all will be well. We must, of course, expect that this will take some time. Possible even a few months, but it will be time well spent.

The final scenario, that of a rapid, almost exponential growth in the number of certificates because someone has decreed that the organisation shall embrace the DevOps philosophy, is perhaps the trickiest of all to manage. Partly because going down this road does itself immediately throw the organisation into a state of flux as regards both existing and new applications. Furthermore, the brave new DevOps world will itself be a challenge for all of the development and support personnel, before they even think about certificates and PKI. Suddenly, their ordered world of developing and deploying applications according to a proven model is thrown into chaos. Now, everything is going to be microservices running in kubernetes or containers, according to an operational mode which is quite foreign to them. If they are moving to the cloud at the same time, which they probably will be, then there will be a raft of new challenges to embrace which simply did not exist before. Once they have finally worked out how their particular cloud space is going to operate and have put in place all of the structured components necessary to run things in their containers, they then have to learn about code repositories, automated manifests and all sorts of other paraphernalia which they did not previously need. Then, when it does not function as expected (which will definitely be the case), they will have to learn about and deploy a service mesh, within which they will find a very basic certificate authority which will certainly be non-compliant with their own enterprise certificate authority and, in any event, they will have little or no visibility of the resultant certificates as they are created and destroyed automatically. And that is just for self-signed certificates. What about trusted third-party certificates? Ah! A good question which at this stage, no one will have mentioned. And so, they will be tempted to buy yet another layer which integrates with the service mesh and offers a better visibility of these certificates, together with a more robust link to trusted third-party certificate suppliers. While they are grappling with all of this, the core PKI team will come along and ask them to demonstrate how their new certificates are going to comply with organisational policies. Naturally, they will not have a clue. There is a good deal of work required here and it will not be easy. Furthermore, the costs, in relation to third party–supplied certificates will rise sharply, and this will need to be explained to management. The primary problem, however, will be one of complexity. Firstly, if the organisation is foolish enough to go down this road when they already had a perfectly good infrastructure in place, together with a perfectly good application development and deployment methodology, then they will be introducing an immediate security risk, which will manifest itself in various ways. Consider firstly the personnel situation. Under the DevOps banner, operational and support staff will be shed while developers of a different persuasion will be required to follow the new model. This will cause an immediate, and severe, personnel crisis. Good skills, won, in some cases, over decades, will walk out of the door and be lost forever. *That* is a security risk as only those individuals really knew how everything was configured and how it interacted as an organisational system. Once lost, those skills will be difficult, if not impossible to replace. Those accountants who believe that outsourcing is the answer are living in a different world. Then, having resized and reorganised the IT development and support personnel, the new working model has to be defined. By who exactly? A new group of managers perhaps? What experience have they of the organisational IT estate and how it functions? The answer will be none. *That* is a security risk as these people may well overlook important factors which remain in place during the transition to the DevOps model. The new staff may think that they know all about this new way of going about things and they will, no doubt, be familiar with all the buzzwords and politically correct nomenclature. The truth is that they will not have much experience at all and that they will certainly not understand precisely how all of these layers are working. Indeed, the suppliers don't understand it themselves, as the author discovered while researching for this book. No, the newly formed development team will not really understand how all of this works. *That* is a security risk, as they will likely make serious errors in their coding, especially with regards to communications. Furthermore, as they progress quickly (which they will be desperate to do, in order to show how marvellous this new model is), certificates and PKI will be the last thing on their minds. *That* is a security risk as they will not understand what is happening with their certificate estate. On top of all of this, the poor PKI core team must try to interact with these inexperienced developers, working amid a technical landscape which they do not understand, and get them to follow policies and procedures with respect to certificates which, most of the time, they have no knowledge of and have certainly never seen. *That* is a security risk as the entire certificate estate for the organisation is effectively out of control. Got the picture? Yes, that's right, going down this road makes no sense whatsoever if you already have your own internal infrastructure, supported by your own people who know it like the back of their hands. The advocate's argument will be, "ah! but this lets us develop code quickly and put things up into the live environment two or three times a day". Why on Earth would you want to do that? A good question. Suffice it to say that if the organisation is suddenly struck with this scenario, then they are in real trouble. It will not be unrecoverable, but it will be super expensive, highly troublesome and, for quite a long period, will expose the organisation to security risks which they were not previously experiencing. The answer will be to try, as far as is possible, to limit the amount of inter- and extra-container communication that is occurring and to try to ensure that your cloud landscape is sufficiently wide not to allow for automated load balancing among containers. On top of this, it will be necessary to have an extremely strict set of policies around application development, test and deployment, which effectively slow down the process and force people to think carefully about what they are doing. A dedicated PKI layer might well need to be emplaced. Needless to say, the PKI policy and operational documents will all need to be updated, and this will need to be communicated across the entire organisation, not a task for the faint-hearted. The irony is that, having gone down this road and spent an absolute fortune in doing so, what can your applications, and therefore your organisation, do which it could not previously do? The answer is, nothing at all. Furthermore, in the process, the organisation would have given away all of its priceless data and effectively lost control of its IT estate completely, as well as losing key, irreplaceable personnel. The Emporer's new clothes look lovely, don't they?

SUMMARY

Within this section, three different, but quite typical, scenarios have been explored, each of which would have an impact upon the organisational PKI. The nature of this impact varies from predictable and controllable, to completely chaotic and very worrying from a security and compliance perspective. Suggestions have been made as to how a core PKI team might cope with each of these scenarios and, from these suggestions, the nature of the scenarios themselves becomes clear. Having this sort of foresight is essential when it comes to effectively managing a PKI. Such a foresight should also be integrated into the organisation's disaster recovery plan. In any event, growth is a phenomenon that needs to be carefully understood from an IT management perspective and, especially, from the perspective of managing a PKI.

Chapter 19

What happens if we acquire other companies?

Merging public key infrastructures

When a merger or acquisition takes place, we are struck with the reality of two sets of systems which must, in theory at least, operate under one banner. There exist a plethora of items that must be attended to and, one may safely guarantee, the Directors and Senior Managers will be preoccupied in the organisational hierarchy and who gets which position. They are not going to be particularly interested in public key infrastructure (PKI). Indeed, most of them will never have heard of it. The bigger question at this juncture will be how the two branches of the organisation will operate. Even though they have come under the same administration, they may continue to operate as two distinct entities, at least for a time. Alternatively, the decision may have been taken early on that they will operate as one, with a single organisational hierarchy and one common direction. If this is the case, then there will be much on the agenda for rationalisation, including financial management, human resources and, of course, the core activity of the new combined operation. Sorting through all of this is likely to take some time and so, it is equally likely that, for a while, the two IT operations will continue to function more or less as they were.

Somewhere along this time line, it will occur to the new directorate that the two IT operations could also usefully be rationalised into one, with a common direction. It is likely that one of these departments will be the larger, stronger partner, or perhaps, simply the better organised partner and, no doubt, a decision will be made to model the new IT operation loosely on this example. There shall, no doubt, be an attendant reshuffle of personnel, especially at the higher levels, and this will take a little while to consolidate and to be communicated throughout the organisation. Once this position has been reached, then the core PKI team of the stronger component may also take steps to start planning a sensible consolidation of that particular function. Indeed, it is likely that the core team itself will have undergone some changes in its personnel line up, possibly absorbing one or two new members from the other side. And there is always a certain amount of company politics to absorb, together with, no doubt, some strongly held views from either side. However, once this has settled down and they have got to know each other and how they have been working, a proper plan may be drawn up with which to proceed.

A sensible first step would be to gather together all of the operational policies and procedures, liaising closely with the (also consolidated) Information Security department, to ensure that they make sense from the perspective of the new organisation. Probably, there will be some very good points within both sets of policies, and these will need to be carefully considered in light of the new operation and its stated direction. This may be an iterative process as, at each stage, it may be found that one or more of the policies is simply unworkable within the new organisation. Or it may be that the policies and procedures being discussed don't quite meet the security and compliance requirements for the new organisation. So, there will be much to discuss. However, it will be important not to get bogged down in these discussions. Decisions must be made, for better or worse, and things must be moved along at a reasonable pace, in order that progress be made. It will always be possible to fine tune these things at a later date, but a starting position must be arrived at in good time, in order that the real integration work may progress.

Once the policies and procedures have been decided and clearly documented, they must also be communicated to all concerned. This will include the developers, support staff and anyone who has anything whatsoever to do with the PKI. Consequently, a proper communications plan must be drawn up and enacted without delay. In parallel with this activity, an operational project plan must be drawn up for the migration of the combined infrastructure to this new model. If the policies and procedures are little changed from those of the stronger side, then that will certainly simplify matters. If this is not the case, then the migration project will be quite extensive, but certainly not impossible to undertake. The plan itself is the key to a smooth migration. If it follows a systematic methodology, with periodic checks along the way, then all should be well. Indeed, it should be a matter of pride among the new team to get this all working smoothly and efficiently.

The project plan will need to use, as a starting point, an architectural map of both sets of infrastructure, whether in-house or third-party hosted or both. It may well be discovered that, in this context, one side is better documented than the other and that there will need to be an alignment. This will require a certain amount of discussion and discovery, but it should not be too onerous a task. And, of course, the documentation should, itself, be to a particular standard with templates used that everyone concerned may readily understand. Eventually, the core PKI team should reach the point where it is satisfied that it understands precisely what it has, and must therefore administer, in terms of infrastructure. A way must now be found of working systematically through this infrastructure in order to bring everything in line with the new policies and procedures. One way of doing this would be to construct a simple relational database whose primary table contains every server, with the next layer representing every certificate on that server, exactly where it is stored and what its purpose is. This information may be cross referenced with applications in order that no stone is left unturned. Of course, this might be further complicated by the near certainty that there will also be some application rationalisation occurring. Still, one has to start somewhere and be prepared to, occasionally, go back over previously covered ground, in order to ensure that everything is accounted for. Yes, this is a little complicated, but it would surely not be expected that it would be too easy.

Once this plan has been activated, progress may swiftly be made if different segments of the plan are entrusted to defined teams assembled from the development and support personnel. They may each be allocated a section of the infrastructure, in order that some parallel processing may be undertaken in order to get things under proper control. Of course, they must understand what they are looking for and how to correct things as they go. For this, proper and detailed instructions must be supplied by the core PKI team. The latter will be constantly checking the work that has been undertaken and satisfying themselves that all is well. After a little while, progress will be seen to be being made and the whole task will start to appear less daunting. Indeed, it would probably be found that certain of the developers will really warm to the task and apply themselves to it with an appropriate zeal. They may also be a healthy spirit of competition that develops between the various teams, ensuring that the task is properly undertaken.

There is a parallel activity here which will mainly be the preserve of the core PKI team, and that is to ensure that all of the certificate information and associated changes are reflected within the certificate management database. This could be a little tricky as the junior partner will have had some sort of certificate database itself. This may have been developed in-house or it may have been a bought-in ready-made product. Either way, certificates will need to be exported from that database to the one being maintained by the core team. If the junior database is a commercially sourced item, there may be some associated support issues and the supplier concerned is unlikely to be especially sympathetic to the cause. There will no doubt be all manner of complicated exit clauses within the contract, which the core PKI team, together with the purchasing department, shall have to address, while all the time keeping things visible and actively managed.

This rather complex mix of activities would no doubt buzz along for some time, until a point is reached when the core PKI team may declare itself satisfied that all is aligning properly with policy, that all is visible and that all is being actively managed. If there is third-party infrastructure involved, this will be a complex matter. Furthermore, the Information Security department shall need to be equally satisfied from a security and compliance perspective. This latter point will become increasingly troublesome, the more that third-party infrastructure is used. Suppliers may glibly declare that their infrastructure is fully compliant with this and that, but the

Information Security team will want to be able to demonstrate this for themselves. At least, they will if they are doing their job properly which, we shall assume, they are, but they will also have been amalgamated in some way or another. Indeed, under such scenarios, there would be a good deal of human resource reallocation and, where appropriate, retraining. Consequently, many areas within the organisation will be in a state of flux. However, from the PKI perspective, things must, of course, continue to operate properly throughout all of these changes. The organisation will not want to experience IT outages while the two IT departments come together. This brings to the fore the need for clarity with respect to roles and responsibilities within the PKI landscape. As long as the core PKI team is quickly defined and emplaced, the other areas may be brought into alignment via the departments concerned.

When all of these areas have been attended to, and only a sub-section has been mentioned here, then the new organisational PKI should be running smoothly. All certificates should be compliant with a defined specification, whether self-signed or supplied by trusted third parties, and all should be registered within the certificate database which, in turn, should automatically be monitoring expiry dates and sending messages to the appropriate departments. If there have been significant personnel changes, then this database shall have to be updated in order to reflect these changes with respect to roles and responsibilities within the PKI sphere. In particular, the names of those responsible for certificates must be brought up to date.

The primary issue with all of this is that, in the case of a merger or acquisition, there will be so much activity rippling through the new organisation, that no one is going to be particularly interested in the PKI. There will likely be a raft of changes among the executive positions and, quite possibly, whole departments may be created or closed down. There may also be staff redundancies and new terms and conditions of employment for at least some of the workforce. Some will be happy with their new lot. Others less so. But the PKI must be kept going in spite of all of these changes. Consequently, it will be a very challenging time for the core PKI team, with much work to undertake, mostly without recognition and, sometimes, against a backdrop of ill will. This is where good management skills will be required. The detail of the various tasks may be unravelled, documented and set in motion, but there will remain a reliance upon developers and support staff from both sides of the organisation. Furthermore, it may be that a number of these individuals will be unknown to the core team and so it will be necessary to conduct a degree of team building as the initiative progresses. An important detail that the core PKI team must get right is communication to the Directors and Senior Managers throughout the new organisation. They must be brought to an understanding as to the importance of the PKI for the ongoing smooth management of the new organisation and its operational activities. Of course, they will know how to do this if they built the original PKI themselves and undertook a communications exercise at that time.

SUMMARY

In this section, a closer look has been taken at what it means for the organisational PKI when two or more entities come together as a result of mergers and acquisitions. It has been shown that a systematic, methodical approach will be required in order to merge the certificate estate and bring it under a common management model. Furthermore, this would need to be undertaken in close synchronisation with the Information Security team (who will also have undergone major changes) as policies and procedures from the various different sectors are examined and refined. It is not easy to apply any sort of meaningful metric to this, as so much depends upon how diverse the organisations were prior to their coming together. Typically, it will be found that one of the parties is better organised than the other(s) and that *their* policies and procedures actually fit the other organisation quite well. However, they still have to be implemented and that will be a significant and quite complex task. It is all achievable though, and with keen observation, good planning and good management, there is no reason why it should not all be undertaken smoothly and efficiently.

Chapter 20

Who should be responsible for it all?
Accountability

It has been stressed that a public key infrastructure (PKI) is an essential component within any organisation that is operational within the modern world. Almost every undertaking, whether commercial, governmental or academic, is underpinned by IT and, in turn, that IT, in the modern world, relies very much upon the associated PKI. Consequently, as an entity, it is one of the key components supporting the organisation, no matter what that organisation is. Ultimately, accountability must lie with the Chief Executive Officer, Minister, Dean or whoever is heading up the organisation. Of course, they will not understand, and not want to understand, the technical detail, but they must be made aware of how important the PKI is overall. Such an understanding will, in turn, allow them to make sensible decisions in this context. And from there, responsibility and accountability must flow down through every layer of organisation and administration. It may be the core team who is administering things on a day-to-day basis, but the PKI touches everyone and they must all play their particular part.

As stated, ultimately, accountability rests at the very top. If the PKI fails completely, this person, whoever they are, must account for themselves and explain why. In order to be able to do this, they must remain informed. Consequently, it is a duty of the core PKI team to ensure that anything significant in this context is reported back up the chain of command, right to the top. The importance of the PKI to the organisation demands nothing less. This top person (a CEO by any other name) may then question the bevy of directors, ministers or academics, immediately beneath them, in order to understand the situation and to get things moving if action is required. It follows then that those in the ultimate leadership position must be aware of the PKI, any significant changes or challenges affecting it and, naturally, its ongoing importance to the organisation.

Immediately beneath this position exists the army of directors, ministers or their equivalents, who are responsible for specific areas or functions within the organisation. Their immediate view will be that the PKI is an IT entity and therefore nothing to do with them. Indeed, nothing is further from the truth. The PKI underpins almost every activity in which they are

DOI: 10.1201/9781003360674-20

engaged, one way or another. If it stops working, it will definitely impact upon their department, whatever that department is. Furthermore, the staff within the department will often be directly affected by any failures within the PKI. If they wish their department to be well run, then they must be aware of this and given at least a basic understanding of what the PKI actually is. Yes, they are responsible and accountable. It is *their* department. In addition, they are responsible for the smooth, day-to-day, operation of the department and all that entails, including the relevant IT landscape and the PKI. They must therefore make it their business to understand how all of this works, at least at the conceptual level.

Beneath that layer come the executive managers (or equivalents). This layer is important as this is where many of the operational decisions are made. These are the people who often liaise with external consultants from the big technology companies and often believe what they are told by them, without referring to their own people or, very often, without listening to their advice. If these individuals don't really understand the workings of the technology around them, then they are not in a position to make intelligent, rational decisions. This explains why so many bad IT-related decisions are made within organisations, large and small. So, this layer is a real challenge. They should certainly be held accountable for their decisions but, unfortunately, this seems rarely to be the case. In any event, with respect to PKI, it is absolutely essential to ensure that these individuals have a working knowledge of it. Enough to understand what external consultants are talking about and, therefore, to be able to ask the right questions and challenge assumptions. They should always check everything that they have been told with their own people and, with respect to PKI, they should always involve the core PKI team in any discussions around certificate management. If this group of individuals decided to embrace the DevOps and Cloud Native philosophy, for example, how would they be in any position to recommend such a strategy without understanding what impact it would have on the organisational PKI and, therefore, the organisation as a whole? Well, of course. they would not be in a good position to understand the implications and would, therefore, be likely to make poor decisions which would end up costing the organisation a great deal of time and money for no good reason. This scenario, sadly, is quite a common one today. These people should be accountable for the repercussions of any decisions they make, including those which affect the PKI. Consequently, they have a direct responsibility and accountability for the smooth running of the organisational PKI.

Beneath that layer, there is usually a group of section managers or area managers, which may be assigned to particular operational areas. These individuals will, as part of their role, necessarily interface with those who are designing, developing and supporting both applications and the infrastructure upon which they sit. They will also be interfacing with other, general administration and operational staff and shall, consequently, have a pretty good idea of what is going on within their area. As an integral part of this localised knowledge, they should have a good idea of what the PKI is and how it operates within their area. This group should be relatively easy to liaise with as they will be keen to understand how the IT in *their* area is working. They have a broad responsibility for what is happening throughout their area, and so, this must necessarily include a responsibility for their portion of the PKI. If certificates in their area are expiring and breaking connectivity, it is, at least partly, their responsibility to get to the bottom of things and find out what is going on. Naturally, the core PKI team and others will be assisting them in this context.

Beneath this layer, we have the system architects, developers, support staff and project-related personnel who are responsible for creating and maintaining systems and infrastructure. Naturally, they have a direct responsibility for certificate management within their groups and, for the broader PKI, in conjunction with the core PKI team. The developers in particular have some distinct responsibilities. They must, for example, follow the relevant policies and procedures, ensuring that any certificates under their jurisdiction are fully compliant with the same. They must be able to demonstrate to the Information Security folk that this is the case and freely exchange information with this group to ensure that everything stays on track. It goes without saying that this layer is also responsible for renewing certificates as and when appropriate, as well as the creation of new certificates and ensuring that unused or otherwise rogue certificates are properly revoked. They will receive notifications from the certificate management database and will be responsible for responding to them in good time, ensuring that no certificate expires unexpectedly.

The above paragraphs have been making the point that, actually, almost everybody in the organisation has *some* responsibility towards the PKI, while the distinct groups identified here have direct accountability, albeit in slightly different ways. For this desirable state of affairs to exist within any organisation, there must be an 'across the board' understanding, at least in principle, of what the PKI is and why it is so important to the organisation. It follows then, that communication is paramount. Nobody will welcome responsibility for something which they do not understand. The core PKI team has a tough job in this respect, for they will undoubtedly find it difficult to get the ears of some of these individuals. However, they must persist and get the message across, that this thing is important and they should know something about it. Eventually, the message will be absorbed and, hopefully, full support will be given to the core PKI team and sensible decisions will be made higher up the chain.

And so, in answer to the question posed by the title of this chapter, everyone in the organisation has a responsibility to understand what the PKI is and what it does. All those at Director and Senior Manager level are fully accountable for the PKI and its ongoing operation. All those at executive and middle management level are responsible for anything which might impact the PKI, directly or indirectly. Others have a direct responsibility for certificate management within their particular areas. However, those who are accountable must also realise that they are accountable, and so, the aforementioned communications exercise is crucially important. The Information Security team might be good allies in this context, as they will certainly be interested in a smooth-running PKI.

SUMMARY

Responsibility and accountability have been discussed in this section, and it has been suggested that, in fact, almost everyone in the organisation has a duty of care and associated responsibility with respect to the PKI. It has been further suggested that those at the Director and Senior Manager level are directly accountable, even if they are not aware of the fact and that those at the executive level have a duty to acquaint themselves with at least a working understanding of PKI. It is important, and this understanding should inform all of their IT-related decisions. Consequently, good communication is required in order to inform and clarify and, most importantly, make people aware of their own responsibilities in this context.

Chapter 21

PKI, the cloud and the Internet of things

What we should understand

The world has always been in a state of flux due to the machinations of humanity. However, the past two decades have seen things change much more quickly and much more fundamentally. Those who are devoutly religious will no doubt conclude that evil has finally got control of the human race and that this is pushing us towards the judgement day or a self-imposed species extinction. It is not hard to see why such perspectives are surfacing at present. Through massive levels of corruption, power has shifted into the hands of a relatively few giant organisations within each sector and, it is these giant organisations who are effectively running things. The concept of intelligent self-government is simply a token. The real power lies in the hands of the big energy suppliers, the pharmaceutical companies, the highly controlled media and the IT companies. Alongside this operational strength lies the army of accountants, solicitors, barristers and such like who feed off the spoils. This may be a slight simplification, but informed readers will understand the message.

Among these big changes, the cloud and the Internet of things are especially significant. The whole concept of the cloud is an artificial one. For an organisation that has already designed, built and is maintaining a perfectly adequate IT infrastructure, it really makes no sense whatsoever to exchange this model, wherein they had absolute control, for the cloud, within which they do not. Ask any passing five-year old, and they will confirm this wisdom. The arguments that were repeatedly stated within the intense propaganda to use the cloud were mainly centred around ease of deployment. You could deploy a new server very quickly. Oh yes? You could also deploy a new server very quickly upon your own infrastructure. Indeed, wise IT departments would have a number of such servers sitting there ready to be activated at a moments notice. It is not difficult to do this. Furthermore, why were people not questioning the need to create servers quickly? If the relevant internal departments had been doing their jobs properly, there would be absolutely no need as there would have been proper planning, including that of the IT requirement for each department. Furthermore, those with a long experience in IT will understand that it is never a good idea to make

DOI: 10.1201/9781003360674-21

snap decisions and deploy things immediately without first thinking it all through. And, of course, activating a server, itself means nothing, until you associate it with processing tasks of some kind. That means an application, and applications should never be rushed into. If it is simply a question of capacity, then that will have already been covered under capacity planning within a good IT department. If the argument is that the IT department is not good, then moving it into the cloud isn't going to make it any better. No, putting anything at all into the cloud simply does not make any sense. It never did and it never will.

The combination of what people are calling 'cloud native' (which is a completely meaningless tag in itself) and the Internet of things multiplies the situation by making the assumption that everything should be controlled in this manner and, therefore, come under the control of the giant IT suppliers. This is why we have also seen the rise in what has become abbreviated to 'apps'. Everyone has an 'app' for almost anything you can think of and they are nearly all superfluous. But this particular development has been hugely damaging as it has allowed organisations to withdraw physical, tactile, services and replace them with theoretical services which don't provide the same experience and, very often, simply don't work at all, especially if they are reliant upon mobile phones and the associated networks. A good example of this is what has happened with banks. High-street banks have closed down everywhere, so there is no one that you can go and talk to about your account. The telephone service simply doesn't work at all and will drop the line after you have been waiting for 20 or 30 minutes. But there is an 'app' which offers a restricted version of Internet banking, which itself is hugely incompetent and frequently breaks. Consequently, all proper service has been removed and ordinary, decent citizens do not have control over their own finances anymore. How is that an improvement? Well, as any five-year old will tell you, it isn't. But the mechanisms that allow for this are the very things that the cloud native evangelists are crowing about. If you sit down and make a list of all of the services that have been destroyed in the past five or ten years or so, you will soon run out of paper. Technology is damaging society, and therefore civilisation itself, very badly. At the heart of this instrument for damage lies the cloud and the Internet of things, together with all of the fast-changing technologies which are supporting that model. Of course, the same situation is, in parallel, causing a huge erosion in skills as traditional understanding is lost. Often, bluntly so, as many, many thousands of skilled workers are made redundant because organisations are foolish enough to believe the propaganda and embrace these new ideas, usually at a very high cost which, ultimately, gets passed to the consumer. Many of these consumers who were once living a normal life are now living on the breadline. Those that we used to refer to as 'middle class' have become 'lower class', and there is no 'working class' anymore as traditional jobs and the associated skills have all been lost to greed and the evil of automation. Furthermore, if the brave new world supplied by cloud native, containers, service meshes, apps and all the rest of it actually worked, and to the advantage of ordinary, decent folk, then there might be something to it. But it doesn't work. Look around you. Consider all that has been lost. Consider also the almost ubiquitous corruption in both government, commerce, industry and academia. We have certainly entered what the middle kingdom Egyptians predicted as the 'chaos preceding the end of days'. Surely, it is time for people to start waking up to what is going on? You would hope so, but it doesn't seem to be the case. What is happening in the broader world is both reflected in, and to a great extent caused by, IT. Any organisation who seeks to do things properly needs to understand this reality and, consequently, the risks involved in simply swallowing the propaganda and lining up to admire the Emperor's new clothes. Instead, they should take a step or two backwards and repeatedly ask that little question 'why?' In most cases, there will be no answer. In addition, the consequences of going down these roads, especially to skills retention, security and overall manageability should be very carefully considered. And competent leadership will also recognise the value of people. Intelligent, trained individuals who believe in the organisation and try their best to ensure its success, whether offering a public service or providing goods of some kind. When these people are lost, the organisation is weakened. As John Donne said back around 1600, *'Any man's death diminishes me, because I am involved in mankind, and therefore never send to know for whom the bells tolls; it tolls for thee'*. John Donne considered that 'no man is an island' but instead is part of the 'greater continent' of humanity. Consequently, everyone is important. The same may be said of the humanity of the organisational workforce, from the CEO down to the lowest cleaner or manual worker. They are all a part of the continent which represents that organisation. If thousands of them are made redundant at a stroke, the organisation is irrevocably damaged. Outsourcing is not the answer either as this just brings 'foreigners' into the continent who do not understand it or how it works. And, no, they will not have the same skills as those whom they have replaced. *Those* skills will be lost forever and the organisational continent will never be the same again. This is all basic intelligence that should be understood by almost everyone, in every organisation. So, what is going on? A single word. Corruption.

Elsewhere in this book, the advantages of building your own infrastructure using freely available open-source tools has been stressed. If this approach has been taken, then managing a public key infrastructure (PKI) will be straightforward enough. If the chaotic approach depicted above is taken, then, equally, managing the PKI will be difficult. The assumption behind the Internet of things and cloud native computing is that absolutely everything is reduced to a 'thing' which is, in turn, deployed somewhere in the cloud. But what exactly is the 'cloud'? It is not some magic space in the sky where you may safely store all of your data. Neither is it some magic system which is going to somehow boost your organisation's performance overnight, or make you more 'productive' just as all the propaganda keeps telling you. No, all the cloud is, is someone else's infrastructure. It is still server cards mounted in frames with processors on them and arrays of discs or solid-state devices for storage. Will this infrastructure be situated in secure, purpose-built data centres, attended by highly trained, highly skilled staff who have also been security cleared? No, it won't. More typically, it will be built into shipping containers and deployed anywhere in the world where it is cheap to do so. It will be attended to by local, outsourced personnel whom you have never met and who you don't know anything about. The possibility of these individuals being security cleared is practically zero. They will be selected for the task according to cost.

In fact, if you have taken *this* route, you have given away your IT, your IT infrastructure, your related skills and all of your organisation's operational data, together with your intellectual property, into the hands of somebody you don't know who could be anywhere in the world. Having done so, you will pay, for however long your organisation exists, an annual fee which will rise and rise, for absolutely nothing. Whereas, before taking this route, you had no such cost. And yet, you will still need to pay for, usually outsourced, staff to administer this at your end. Does it make any sense at all? Ask the five-year old again.

Having embraced the cloud native, Internet of things approach, there then comes the question of how to design, build and deploy applications into this magic space. This is where the DevOps mentality comes in. Instead of having separate departments to draw up the design specification, build to specification, check the build against the design specification and also for general operability and stability, and, finally, to test and then deploy to the live environment, we have one team called DevOps. This team has an extremely high opinion of itself, based upon the fact that they can construct a simple piece of code and deploy it into the magic space in the same day, or even several times a day. Is this sensible? No, it is not. This is a recipe for disaster as bad code will be regularly finding its way to the live environment which, these days, is usually the public-facing web site. The author has just, prior to writing this paragraph, been attempting to use a banking web site. It repeatedly froze during the identity verification stage. Looking at what was happening behind the scenes in my browser, the routines written for the application were simply colliding with each other and breaking when trying to call the verification service. Bad code. No doubt written by a 'DevOps' team. This experience is not unusual these days. Even when you know that your connection is fast and good, the performance of both commercial and governmental web sites is dire and sometimes quite impossible to use. In the case of banks, having closed the high-street banks, there is nowhere to go. The telephone service does not work at all, and so where does this leave the consumer? Nowhere. Is this good? No, it is not. The brave new world of DevOps on cloud native environments is incredibly clumsy, unreliable and downright bad. What does this mean for a PKI? We shall see.

The reasons for this IT tragedy have been variously covered in previous chapters, but they hinge around the microservices-based architectures with kubernetes, service meshes and the plethora of plug-in tools (including for PKI management) available with which to try to make the whole mess work. If you have thousands of microservices deployed in many hundreds of containers, within an infrastructure which, actually, you know nothing about, other than its theoretical size, then you have a great number of digital certificates to manage. The number may be so great that it is impractical to try to manage them manually, and you will have to turn to yet another layer of automation. This will be difficult to configure, almost certainly unreliable in operation (which is why my bank's web site keeps breaking when trying to make connections) and by no means inexpensive. Alternatively, you could simply throw up your hands in despair and let an external organisation take control of it for you. This latter option is increasingly being taken up, especially among government agencies (who are, of course, being 'encouraged' to do so). This option will be even more expensive, and you will lose even more control over your PKI. You will, in fact, have entrusted everything to an external company whom you know little about, other than what they tell you on their web site, which will be practically nothing. And how will they manage things? Probably, by insisting that you use a particular brand of service mesh, into which they will integrate their own agents with which to monitor the creation and deployment of both self-signed and third party–supplied certificates. If they do this properly, there is no reason why, technically, it should not work. The question is, do you really want all these certificates created automatically, just because some irresponsible developer in 'DevOps' has been putting up repeated builds of the same application? There is a cost implication here of course, as well as one of operational performance which, with all these layers, will simply get worse and worse, as it has with my bank and several other sites which I, unfortunately, need to visit. Suppliers will tell you that there is no performance issue with their part of the service. But what does that mean? Where is the qualification of such claims? There isn't any. There can't possibly be, because they are not your organisation. They do not understand how you operate or who your customers are. The fact is that with a large container-based application, deployed in chunks by developers who are simply 'playing' with their new technology toys, overlaying a PKI and making it work according to any sort of standard is difficult. If your DevOps team is in house, then you at least have the option of requiring them to adhere to a specific group of policies and procedures, some of which may be around frequency of build and deployment, others around building to specifications supplied by a proper project management team. Just letting developers loose within a DevOps model and letting them develop whatever enters their heads is asking for trouble. But this is happening. Indeed, it is being actively encouraged and enthusiastically adopted.

Getting back to the infrastructure, if you have many hundreds of containers, spread across a number of servers (but you don't necessarily know which) and being started and stopped at will by developers, then trying to manage the certificates which they need for communications both between each other and with the outside world is very difficult. Suppliers will crow about automatic 'load balancing'. From where to where and on whose infrastructure? If you have planned things properly, there will be no requirement for load balancing. But your cloud supplier might want to load balance across *his* environment. That, of course, is not your concern, but it will play havoc with your PKI. Certificates will be orphaned at an alarming rate, and there will exist a veritable sea of them out there on your cloud. Furthermore, you will be buying several times more certificates from your trusted third-party providers. If the right level of control and operational rigour is instilled within the development teams, then each team might manage its own certificates and then feedback into the central certificate management database and the core PKI team. This may work, if the teams are very focused and are not throwing up builds several times a day. However, in the longer term, it is likely to become messy. Within such a technical infrastructure, you may have to turn to automation, but *whose* automation? If you are using a service mesh to manage your containers, firstly, ensure that your containers stay put for a while and don't get changed for the sake of change. Secondly, ensure that you have enough capacity not to have to 'load balance' things around. Thirdly, take a close look at the certificate authority (CA) provided by the service mesh and see if you can work with it directly. It should be able to output information directly to your certificate management database and also receive instructions from it. If you can get things configured this way round, so that it is your database which is effectively controlling the issuance and closing of self-signed certificates through the service mesh, then that might work well enough. For trusted third-party certificates, you may also be able to do this, or simply control them directly from the database. It is not an ideal state of affairs, by any means, but it might work well enough in practice, and it would keep you (the core PKI team) in the driving seat. If things have already become so over-complicated and messy that no one knows anything about the certificates being used, then you are in trouble. It is likely that you will have to deploy some sort of third-party tool in order to latch on to your container estate and the service mesh and grab control of the certificates in use. Don't consider for a moment that this will be an easy or straightforward exercise. Many of these tools have yet to be proven in the real world of large-scale operations. Forget what the aggressive and over-confident supplier staff tell you, these things remain in their infancy for the most part. The really big supplier companies will try to convince you to trust them *because* they are really big. It means nothing. They don't really understand this stuff either and are still feeling their way around. Anyone who feels it necessary to employ technology 'advocates' has something to hide. They will simply use your organisation as a test bed for their own, poorly founded, illogical ideas. And you will pay for it. And keep paying for it.

Alternatively, you could build your own in-house IT infrastructure again, develop things intelligently with proven development languages and design, construct and manage your own PKI with your own, well-trained staff who, by the way, shall be delighted to work for you and do their best to support the organisation. Now, ask the five-year old about *that!*

So, the Internet of things and the cloud native DevOps way of doing things may provide toys for developers to play with, but it does not necessarily bring much to your organisation. If you do go down this road, there is no coming back, at least not without a struggle. If you do this *and* outsource your own IT staff, then you have given away the crown jewels of your organisation. Directors who make such decisions will have to live with the consequences of them. One such consequence is that your organisational PKI will likely be in a complete mess. If you finally outsource this as well, then you have really lost control of much of your organisation, whether it be a government ministry, commercial enterprise or academic institution. Fortunately, there are other ways of looking at the situation and you could, with a little effort, get it all nicely back under your own direct control. The irony is that this latter tactic costs virtually nothing while the former one will gobble up large chunks of your operational capital. In any event, you need to know what is happening with your PKI. If someone else is managing it for you, then ask them. They should be able to show you where every single certificate is, tell you who issued it, when and what it does. They should also be able to provide you with a list of certificates due to expire within the next three months. Ask them for it. If they cannot provide these answers, then, what are they doing? And why are you paying them for it?

SUMMARY

In this section, the Internet of things, the cloud native way of doing things and the cloud have been discussed and placed within a proper perspective. The benefits of different approaches to application development have similarly been discussed and some very pertinent questions have been asked in this context. The subject of outsourcing has arisen, and this has been discussed with respect to the impact upon organisations who pursue such a policy. It has been shown that, in real terms, the cost of adopting these new technologies is very high, both financially and in other ways. There are reasons why this is the case, and some of these have been elucidated here.

Chapter 22

PKI and the global financial industry

The reliance upon a large-scale public key infrastructure

We live in a world of increasing buzzwords, trends and fashions which, unfortunately, people follow like sheep, afraid to stand out from the herd, even when the herd is stupid, or worse, malicious. Individuals lack moral courage and simply go with the flow, admiring the Emperor's new clothes, which have been described and modelled by those wishing to seize control. Consequently, corruption is running wild, like it has never done before, and our world is being taken over by a relatively small number of entities who wield enormous power. Information Technology is enabling this transformation in two ways: firstly, it is repeatedly coming up with new methodologies and technologies which are effectively meaningless but will, nevertheless, distract both individuals and organisations, soaking up enormous amounts of time, energy and, of course, cost. Secondly, beneath this frivolous layer of new technologies and buzzwords, to which everybody seems to believe that they must conform, there is the real layer which is systematically taking control. This is implemented in various ways, which are outside the scope of this particular work, but experienced professionals in many fields will understand this reality.

An important and potentially worrying example of such developments is that of decentralised finance (DeFi). Even a single, unambiguous definition of the term eludes us at present, as it obviously means different things to different people, but of one thing you can be sure, both the criminal fraternity and established organisations will be looking to make money out of the situation and, if somebody makes money, then somebody else is losing it, and that somebody else will be, in the end, the man in the street. When government agencies or large organisations suffer fraud, they simply pass on the cost to the consumer. This will likely happen quite often as the concept of decentralised finance takes hold. In order to understand the potential for chaos and fraud, it is necessary to understand how such a scheme would work in practice and this is something which has confused almost everyone who is promoting the idea. The truth of this becomes obvious when a little research is undertaken and some of the claims being made by enabling

DOI: 10.1201/9781003360674-22

companies are examined more closely. This isn't easy to do, as none of the so-called 'suppliers' actually tell you what they are doing. The big technology suppliers fall back on buzzwords and so-called use-cases, often presented by unlikely looking individuals who cannot speak English properly, so further obscuring the case. One thing is for sure however, and that is that public key infrastructure (PKI) has a significant part to play, however the situation develops.

The concept of Blockchains is a good place to start because, this is one of the so-called enabling technologies which is, itself, adorned with further buzzwords such as 'fabrics' and other meaningless terms. Furthermore, any definition of Blockchains will usually make some fundamental errors around how technology is actually working. The concept sounds simple enough. 'Blocks' are data containers of a finite size which, when filled, are replaced by the next block, which is linked to the previous block with a time and date stamp, and so on, creating a chain of blocks which may hold any sort of information. In addition, when each block is filled, a hash is taken of it and compared each time the block is read, in order to ensure that nothing has been changed within the block. A Blockchain is thus often described as an immutable, read-only ledger and, consequently, compared with a traditional relational database is supposed to be more secure or 'trustworthy'. There are several things wrong with such a definition and, therefore, the actuality of Blockchains. Firstly, the idea that such a model is somehow better because it is 'distributed'. Well, all that really means is that, in theory at least, the Blockchain database (for that is what it is) resides upon more than one physical machine. It may be that it resides simply upon two mainframes, situated in different states or, possibly, different countries, but they may still be owned by the same company. This could be the case, even if they were on 20 physical machines. The fact is that, as a user, you have no idea what or where these machines are, who owns them and who is administering them. But *someone* is administering them and this person effectively has access to your data, however it is stored. That brings a big question to the idea of trust. With respect to blocks, even if there is a hash associated with each one when it has been filled, I could, as an administrator, simply replace ten blocks and ten hashes with new ones and ensure that the date and time stamps align. If I know where everything is and the operational model, nothing is impossible. The negative comparison with relational databases is also misplaced. As a database administrator, I could ensure that tables, or even individual records, are read only and therefore not easily changed. I could also ensure that tables do not grow beyond a certain number of records before creating new ones with a sensible naming convention which includes a time and date stamp. I could also hide them from view and encrypt them for storage. In short, I could make a relational database every bit as secure as a Blockchain, so there is really no advantage to rushing into this new technology, except, of course, that *someone* is set to make big money from it. And you don't have to look far to see who that is.

Then, there is the concept of Blockchain communities which, frankly, is bizarre. One 'advantage' often quoted is that user communities have to be constructed from individuals who are invited, or have to seek permission to join the community. This is proposed as enhancing trust. Oh yes! The fact that someone needs to ask to join the community does not mean that you can trust them. In most cases, you will have absolutely no idea who they really are as pseudonyms are also encouraged. So, your 'trusted' community might well be a group of fraudsters with criminal records who you are going to allow access to your private details and transactions, including financial transactions. Compare that to users of a conventional relational database where each user will need to be granted access by the database administrator who, in turn, will be following a series of security protocols and procedures. Another issue here is that, from either an organisational or personal perspective, if you are already dealing with people whom you trust, then you already have the means to deal with them in place, so why do you need another mechanism which exposes you to fraud? Whichever way you look at it, either from the technical perspective or from a practical, operational perspective, the Blockchain model does not make much sense. A distributed, read-only ledger of all of your transactions, bundled in with those of others, is not necessary. Those involved in an operational supply chain can already track the movement of physical goods, and the same thing pertains with logical transactions such as financial events. There is simply no need to build yet another, parallel infrastructure upon which to echo this information. It is, in fact, a huge security risk. In any event, the construction of a Blockchain will rely heavily upon a PKI. However, if the thing really is distributed across tens or even hundreds of nodes, perhaps in different countries, with the hardware owned by dozens of different entities, then who assumes responsibility for the PKI? Individual members of the Blockchain cannot do so as they have no knowledge of the infrastructure. Only those supplying the hardware could achieve this but, if they are supposed to be unknown to each other, then how is this going to work? Well, it might be automated with discovery and self-signed certificates, but even then, who owns the certificate authority? If web access is granted to anything, then public facing certificates will be required, but who will provision and pay for these when everything is supposed to be anonymous? If all of this sounds a little messy, that's because it is.

An important issue here is that Blockchain technology underpins the entire crypto-currency model. The very idea of an intermediate, unreal currency is itself very questionable. Even more questionable is the amount of fraud which has already been discovered in this area with, no doubt, a great deal more to come. It is not hard to understand why. There is much propaganda around how easy it is to make money in this field, enticing the unwary to invest in crypto-currencies. Furthermore, there are a large number of 'funds' apparently dealing in these unreal currencies, which are traded in something akin to a parallel stock exchange which, in turn, is tied in with

DeFi. Confusing? Well, it all really amounts to the same thing. An IT-related platform which is touted as being trustworthy when, in fact, it is not as, to have trust, you need to really understand what is happening behind the scenes. The Blockchain concept does not allow for this and, in any event, does not provide anything that you could not achieve with a well-designed relational database, despite certain claims to the contrary by those with a vested interest in supplying Blockchain-related technology. On top of this lies the idea of DeFi, which is a way of allowing two or more trading partners to exchange funds directly, thus bypassing the banks. They do this using crypto-currencies. No one mentions that any sums saved in bank fees are more than outweighed by the cost of entering the Blockchain model and, on top of that, you have the costs of moving to and from crypto-currencies. The impression is constantly given of people making fortunes by investing in crypto-currencies and associated funds but, as has been noted, if one party makes money, then another party is losing money to the same degree. Consequently, the probability of losing money by investing in Blockchain and crypto-currencies is at least 50%. In fact, it is probably much higher due to the massive amounts of fraud which have already been uncovered, plus the cost of getting involved in it in the first place. As usual, the winners will be the giant corporations and the losers will be the small and medium-sized enterprises and, ultimately, the consumer. The wonder is that there is already a very significant presence in this world and, naturally, the big technology suppliers are encouraging everyone to go down this road.

DeFi is another interesting factor with respect to PKI. For DeFi to work, there has to be a robust infrastructure to which all parties may subscribe. Now, this could simply be their own existing infrastructures, communicating with each other via a virtual private network. For this, they require the Transport Layer Security (TLS) handshake and the exchange of valid certificates. Therefore, each party must maintain their own, robust PKI. However, if this is sitting upon a distributed Blockchain structure, then ownership becomes a thorny issue. There is already a substantial industry here with a DeFi index where one may check the performance of individual funds or the whole, see the illustrations below.

From Figure 22.1, it may be seen that there are some fairly dramatic fluctuations within this view of the overall DeFi index.

In Figure 22.2, it may be observed that individual funds are also subject to wild variations. In this case, anyone who invested at the high points will currently be feeling a little disappointed. But precisely where has this value gone to? Where has this crypto-currency been flowing into and out of in order to cause these fluctuations?

In Figure 22.3, we can see that very substantial amounts of money have suddenly disappeared and that, from that point onwards, the picture becomes steadily worse. But all of that money is somewhere or has been used for something. Those who have invested in the same had better be pleased with this, assuming of course, that they even understand it.

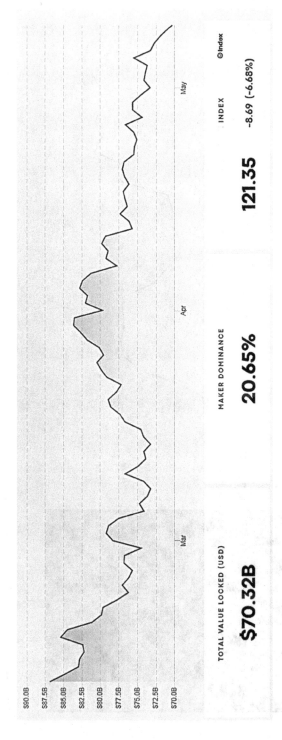

Figure 22.1 An overall DeFi index.

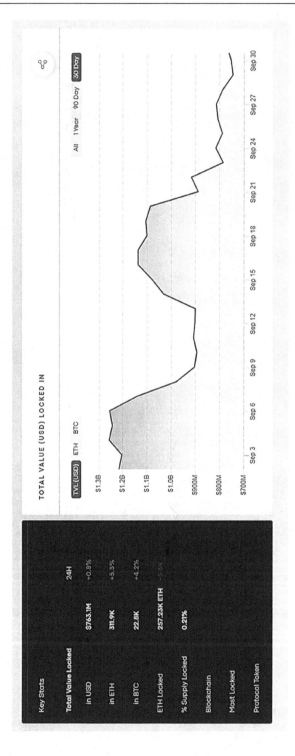

Figure 22.2 An individual fund index.

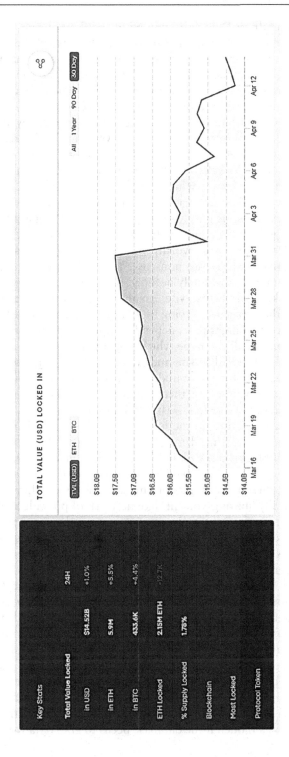

Figure 22.3 Another individual fund.

There is much talk of DeFi undermining the banks and thus saving bank fees. However, one may rest assured that the big banks will be involved in this. And as for crypto-currencies, well, every time they are bought, sold or exchanged, *somebody* makes money on the transaction and *somebody* loses money on the transaction. The latter will always be the consumer. So, the model is really quite similar to the traditional banking model, it is just that it is in someone else's hands. However, it is underpinned by technology (Blockchains) which has been seriously over hyped and misrepresented and this remains the case as this is written. There is nothing magic, or even particularly clever about Blockchains. They are a data collection and harvesting method, enabled by software which, itself, is running upon conventional computer hardware. The idea that this is distributed and therefore anonymous is nonsense. *Someone* knows exactly where everything is and how it is connected. That will be the company trying to sell you a Blockchain-related product. The idea that it is trustworthy because users must register, but they can register anonymously, is also nonsense. You will be dealing with people about whom you know absolutely nothing. If you wanted to deal with people who you do know and trust, you can already do so. So, there is no need for the thing in the first place. Trying to manage a PKI within a Blockchain environment may be a nightmare, depending upon who owns it (and don't believe for a moment all the hype which suggests that *you* own it. You do not). If the supplier has lied to you and, actually, all the hardware is owned by them and there are far fewer nodes than they have led you to believe, which will probably be the case, then they may at least be able to manage a reasonable PKI upon their own infrastructure. If, on the other hand, it really is a distributed architecture, in the hands of many people, then we have a problem, as *someone* will need to take overall responsibility for the PKI. Presumably, each Blockchain will, in fact, have a leading organisation looking after their IT and the associated PKI. They may have been the originator. In which case, it is really up to them to manage the PKI. If they have put in place a dynamically shifting 'torrent' like network of possible nodes which may be either up or down at a given point in time, then they will have to have an equally dynamic PKI which can track such alterations to the virtual network. This is another area where, for many, it will be tempting to fall back on microservices, kubernetes and service meshes, upon which they will then overlay the Blockchain environment. It all gets very complicated indeed and it is all unnecessary. If one wanted a transaction database which was read only to a defined set of users, and whose data was encrypted and signed, it is perfectly possible to build one with either open-source components or with a proprietary system. On such a database, it will be possible to construct custom views in order to decide who can see what, it is equally possible to lock the tables for a read-only snapshot and (far easier than with Blockchains) it is possible to generate almost any report you can think of from the underlying data. Furthermore, you can implement strong access control upon such a model. If the database needs to grab data from multiple sources, you will know exactly where these sources are and will therefore be able to construct a solid PKI around the whole thing. Of course, you can also link it directly to payment clearing houses. So, why do we need anything else? We don't. But many individuals of questionable ethics are making big money out of Blockchains, crypto-currencies and DeFi. And these people are not really thinking about PKI. In which case, that places your transactions at further risk. If you do become involved in any of these initiatives, do ask who is looking after the PKI. If a small group of individuals or organisations were to decide to build such a network, then it would be best to build it themselves using open-source products and, as part of the architectural design, assign one of the parties involved to be responsible for the PKI. That party must then acquaint themselves with every single node on the network, understand where it's certificate stores are and, if everyone in the group is happy with the notion of self-signed certificates, establish an enterprise certificate authority and a certificate management database from where all may be managed. If a web interface is involved, then it will be necessary to use third party–supplied certificates. Alternatively, it would be possible to simply buy the services of a Blockchain technology supplier and trust that they will somehow manage all of this for you. That, however, would be expensive and, by its very nature, insecure.

SUMMARY

In this section, we have had a very quick exposure to the world of Blockchains, crypto-currencies and DeFi. These are all factors which the financial industry, as it stands today, needs to be wary of. More likely, it will embrace the underlying technologies and so attempt to qualify them. However, the underlying technologies are flawed and, in particular, few in this space are really thinking about putting in place a robust PKI. For consumers, dabbling in this area is akin to walking through a minefield. Many are being fleeced and fraud is rife. It may be some years before this situation improves. When it does, we shall have probably lost access to many of our traditional finance industry entities. This factor should be taken into serious consideration, including by the banks themselves, who will be looking for a way to become involved in the broader model.

Chapter 23

PKI and government legislation

Ensuring that legislation is compatible

Finding a starting place when trying to unravel government policy on public key infrastructure (PKI), or what sort of a national PKI might be in place, is sometimes not so easy. Most countries have a security agency, and this is a good place to start as they, at least, will have a good understanding of how a PKI works and will probably have some well-documented guidelines, if you can find them. In the UK, the National Cyber Security Centre has some excellent guidance on setting up a privately hosted PKI. It also offers advice on how to use the various principles discussed, including warnings and design trade-offs. This represents an excellent resource for those who are setting up a PKI for the first time or who just wish to check their own thinking on the subject. Also, in the UK, HM Land Registry offers some guidance and general information appertaining to the PKI which it operates itself. To what extent this would be applicable to an independent organisation, they would have to decide themselves, but there is some good background information there. Staying in the UK, the NHS (National Health Service) has a set of fairly brief guidelines linked to various statement and policy documents, but it must be noted that this refers to NHS policy, *not* UK government policy. One of these policy documents, selected at random, had had 26 revisions to date. This tells me that something is not quite right here, and it is probably a question of the NHS working with third-party suppliers who are lobbying to ensure that their particular products fit the bill. Certainly, working through these documents and guidelines, one gains the impression that they are unnecessarily verbose and, in fact, not too informative. Still, at least, they are aware of what a PKI is. The Ministry of Justice has some available guidance littered with links to various Internet Engineering Task Force (IETF) documents and Government Functional Standards which, together, describe various standards but none of which defines any clear-cut policy. One could trawl through various other ministries and departments and find some good information, but nothing which seems to tie everything together under a national policy, describing what both the present and future should look like. Furthermore, there is no acknowledgement of some of the new technologies and practices which have been discussed within the pages of this book.

DOI: 10.1201/9781003360674-23

In Canada, there is a published set of guidelines which discuss security at a high level and, while mentioning digital certificates, does not really go in to any detail around establishing, using and managing a PKI. There are links to a multitude of other documents which are described as 'policy' documents but which really say nothing except follow best practice, although what that actually is, is anyone's guess. Under 'operational guidance', mention is made of an 'ICM Common Services CA', but how you would find it and access it is another matter. Presumably, if you were within an applicable government agency, you would know about such things and be able to interface with whatever is actually in place. The guidance goes on to mention a list of items which should be adhered to, but it doesn't actually provide them. In other words, it is all very theoretical and politically correct, but there is no detail and nothing to really guide people through the process. However, moving to the province of British Columbia, there is a very good document issued by The Office of the Chief Information Officer which provides a full coverage of both purpose and the necessary standards with which to comply. Excellent, this is exactly what is required for people to reference. It is also notable that the University of British Columbia publishes an Information Security Standard M7 on Cryptographic Controls. This covers practically everything with a nice section on key management and several links to other, interesting documents. It seems as though British Columbia is on the ball here. Moving across to Saskatchewan, they have a host of policies, but I could find nothing on PKI. In Alberta, the Information Management and Technology department has a wealth of information, including strategic planning and the use of various communications technologies. It also has a cyber security strategy which references various broader standards. However, there seemed to be nothing which offered guidance in setting up a PKI. This was later confirmed in dialogue with them. In Manitoba, there is very good guidance for the Manitoba Legal Profession, explaining how to use a PKI and how to manage certificates. It is also commendable that, within this main document, roles and responsibilities are clearly outlined. Excellent, even if only specifically addressing the legal profession. In Ontario, there exists a 114-page document which goes into PKI in detail, including roles, responsibilities and accountability, before moving on to a very good technical guide as to how everything should work. This is really good and could be used as a model elsewhere. The Government of Ontario is to be congratulated on their achievement in this context. I will not go through every province, but it is evident that variability exists as you move across provinces, and there is effectively no clear central policy that goes into the necessary technical detail. Canada is a big place and therefore represents an interesting case study in this respect.

In America, we have NIST (National Institute of Standards and Technology), and of course, it has a good focus upon PKI, including practical annual workshops. There is a document which explains public key technology and the Federal PKI Infrastructure, with links to various standards where applicable. Somewhere, within the NIST documentation, you will find everything necessary to design and implement a PKI, but you may have to dig quite deeply into it. The Federal Records Management offers guidance for digitally signed document management which is actually quite good. A 120-page government document on X509 Certificate Policy for the US Federal PKI, Common Policy Framework, has, so far, 36 revisions but does go into some detail on the subject and represents good guidance. In fact, there are a number of such documents which, together, provide a degree of overlap. However, if an organisation wished to be compliant with these recommendations and associated standards, then they would do well to simply trawl through all of them and extract the information they need. In some respects, there is a little too much information of the wrong kind here. Documents which themselves say little but have endless links to other documents and standards are really not that helpful if you are trying to design and build a good PKI. A simple, plain language, step-by-step guide to design and implementation would be much more helpful. Those responsible in the US should take a trip to British Columbia and see how it is done.

In South Africa, there exist a number of documents covering electronic communications, cyber security and related subjects. However, they are mostly framework documents which describe what should be done but not how to do it. They are very officious and voluminous for the most part but hardly convey anything technical. Interestingly, most of these documents seem to have been written in 2015 and, by 2017, they stop altogether. Consequently, one wonders about the level of electronic communications security in that region.

In Australia, Services Australia provides a number of interesting documents on certificates and PKI, although these seem to be aimed mostly at the provision of health care. The documents include policy statements and practice statements and generally describe who does what within these areas and the departments responsible for them. For the broader governmental area, there is the Gatekeeper Public Key Infrastructure Framework and this generally describes who does what, particularly with respect to registration authorities and certificate authorities (CAs). They also have something called VANguard which supplies services for other government agencies, in particular for authentication purposes. Indeed, there are a great many regulations in Australia, most of which are documented to a greater or lesser extent and cross-reference to various standards. However, they could do with a plain language guide with which to step people through when implementing or growing a PKI.

Sailing across to New Zealand, a different picture emerges. There is some very good documentation, in fact, 12 different policy documents covering both hardware and software. There are also lists of valid CA certificates and expired CA certificates as well as certificate revocation lists. This is very much a 'hands on' approach for departmental information security personnel who will appreciate the in-depth coverage of what they need to understand. The currently active certificates may even be opened and installed onto your local device.

As may be seen in Figure 23.1, from New Zealand it is a simple matter to download and install a New Zealand Government certificate to your local machine. This one is valid until 2025.

We could go around the world and find, no doubt, a significant variance upon the real level of knowledge of PKI within government agencies. It is clear that, in some cases, external consultants have simply been brought in to write policy statements which don't actually tell you anything about the infrastructure or how to engage with it. In most countries, you will find some information but will probably have to speak with internal staff in order to get any further. If you have to engage with a government PKI system from your own organisation, they will probably put you in touch with whoever is running their IT for them and you can work together. It is doubtful that many government agencies actually understand what a PKI is and why it is important to them. This is a great shame. The New Zealand

Figure 23.1 A NZ Government certificate.

Government has obviously understood this and top marks to the province of British Columbia in Canada for having the best documentation of all.

This is important for other reasons. First of all, other legislation such as that covering legal affairs and telecommunications. In the UK, there was a Telecommunications Security Bill passed in 2020 together with a lengthy Impact Assessment which speaks a good deal about costs and third-party involvement. It also speaks of third-party incentives and seems more concerned with who should put a 5G network in place across the country, than the detail behind its security. There is a separate paper from the National Cyber Security Centre which is a 'security analysis' for the UK telecommunications industry. This speaks of possible attacks, risks, mitigation and even proposes a scoring system for threat analysis. All well and good, but where is PKI? Neither of these papers acknowledge that there is such a thing as a PKI and that it might well be applicable for the new, expanded 5G network which is supposed to cover all of the UK. For this to work, there will, of course, be a reliance upon cellular technology, but there will also be a network of associated servers, talking to each other almost constantly. These need to be protected. There are many other such bills, from agriculture to education and more. This situation highlights a problem with government bills in general. They are often written by people with little technical knowledge. They understand the buzz words and some of the obvious security risks, but they do not understand how things are really working in the background. This may be found across government agencies in almost every country. It echoes the situation in industry where organisations have simply given up and handed over their IT, and associated assets, to huge third-party companies who, of course, are encouraging them to do so. But PKI is important and it should be important to governments. The appropriate government agency, probably the security services in league with IT services, should be made responsible for all PKI and certificate-related matters and should have clear, unambiguous guidance documents which explain everything for other agencies to easily digest. They will then be in a strong position to build their own, compliant, PKI. Each government should perhaps have a specialist team, much like the core PKI team discussed earlier in this book, who may advise other agencies and departments and offer them as much help as they need in order to bring things under control. We need to have a clear set of policies and procedures. We need a repeatable, solid architecture. We need to embrace the open-source model and use proven infrastructural components. We need to plan. We need to derive order from chaos.

SUMMARY

This section has taken a short look at how governments and government agencies are looking at PKI. Buried within their information archives, there is usually something about PKI, but it is often very generalised in nature and will often be of little help to those trying to implement or replace a PKI. There is a great deal of cross-referencing, often with broken links which fail, and, clearly, those writing the documentation sometimes have little real knowledge of the subject. They hide behind politically correct jargon and yet more links, but don't actually tell you anything. There are some exceptions, as noted, but, in general, the information is at far too high a level. They need to drop the politics and focus upon the practicalities. Then, they really will be serving the common good of the country they represent. At present, government legislation is found wanting in a subject which should be very high on the agenda.

Chapter 24

Consequences

What happens when it all goes wrong

Failure may occur within any IT system, whether it be hardware or software or because of some user interface issue that had not been anticipated. The same is true of a public key infrastructure (PKI) system, but the consequences of failure within such a system may be dramatic. First of all, let us consider the possible causes of failure. Some of these shall be enumerated below:

I. Certificate expiry. Probably, the most common error. Digital certificates have a validation period, and when a certificate has expired, the service that was accessing that particular certificate will react in some way.

II. Misplaced certificates. There may be situations when, for one reason or another, a certificate is not where it should be or, at least, does not appear to be where it should be. For example, the certificate may have been issued and then stored in an incorrect directory location. Perhaps, it was placed in what was assumed to be the main system directory for certificates when, actually, it needed to be within the directory structure of an application.

III. Change of system address. This situation is particularly pertinent to services and applications which have been built and deployed using the 'container' model in the cloud. While a service mesh or dedicated certificate management system should obviate such occurrences, there will be times when some sort of automated load balancing or manipulation of the containers themselves results in certificates becoming aligned with the wrong system address.

IV. Mismanagement of certificate revocation lists, which might result in rogue certificates cropping up or genuine certificates being refused when they shouldn't be.

V. An assumption that self-signed certificates will be accepted by third-party systems. This may be prevalent where multiple builds have been created among a container cluster and a self-signed certificate has crept through when it should have been a commercially issued variety.

VI. Hardware failure. A server or server card may have failed and the i.p. address effectively stalled. This, in turn, might affect a number of certificates that had been associated, either directly or indirectly, with that particular server.

VII. Software failure. If a first-tier software application fails, it may take several certificates with it. Depending upon what action is taken to restore the application, the associated certificates may have become muddled and connecting applications might struggle to work effectively.

VIII. Service failure. In a microservice-based environment, the sheer number of services may be great, certainly in the thousands or maybe even hundreds of thousands. Most of these services will have a certificate associated with them and will be interacting with other services or at a higher application level. When one of the services fails, it may not be immediately apparent, but it might have broader implications.

IX. Certificate management system failure. This is the type of failure that might be elusive at first. For example, if such a system misbehaves because of a software bug and wrongly assigns certificates, it might not be noticed for a while. When it is discovered, it will likely take a good deal of sorting through as the system inventory picture and the operational reality will have become out of synchronisation.

X. Cloud Native failure. This is an interesting possibility. Organisations that have embraced the Cloud Native philosophy will have necessarily changed the way they design, develop and deploy, not only services and applications, but the entire architecture as associated with their particular IT model. The problem is that there is seldom a single view of this broader picture and, when it goes wrong (which it will), it could impact the organisational PKI quite dramatically. If container clusters become misaligned, or service meshes fail or another layer fails to connect properly, or load balancing fails, everything could, quite suddenly, become messy. Furthermore, because it is all in the cloud, the organisation will have no idea where things actually reside. What they thought they had built may have ended up looking somewhat different, especially if multiple developers have been let loose on the whole and encouraged to build and rebuild. They will think that they are safe because everything has been placed in a common service directory/repository, but there are so many layers and add-on services which are virtual rather than real (as implemented in your own hardware infrastructure) that the possibility of errors is significant.

One could continue and probably extend this list almost indefinitely but, suffice it to say, it is entirely possible, if not probable that, within a commercially sized IT infrastructure, there will be failures that impact the organisational PKI in one way or another. As with all such situations, one needs to be aware of the possibilities and have some contingency plan in place. Furthermore, we must not rely solely on automated contingency because this does not always work as expected. We need to be actively monitoring the situation and have a range of possible solutions to any given eventuality. If this sounds a little complex, that's because it is. But this is what IT management entails.

Now, let us turn our attention to the possible implications of failure. These may be more far reaching than might at first be supposed, varying between mild irritation and absolute catastrophe. This reality is another reason why a dedicated and experienced PKI team is really a necessity in relation to a large organisational IT infrastructure, no matter how it is deployed. It used to be the case that people took the view that certificates affect mostly web browsers and so failures were not really that important. However, there are two flaws in this argument. Firstly, it is not just a matter of web browsers but any machine-to-machine communication, and secondly, web browsers have now become an almost ubiquitous portal to the majority of applications as the user interface. Consider a simple financial transaction, such as when a user might pay his or her solicitor (attorney) bill. Typically, the user will be off-loaded from the main web site to a special 'secure payment' portal. That will involve a handshake and the checking of certificates at both ends. Then, the client reference and the invoice reference will be verified. That will require another two data sources to be referenced with the attendant handshakes and certificate checking. Having completed the on-line payment form, the user will then be taken off to a third-party payment clearing function – another handshake and certificate check. The clearing house will then reference the client's bank. Another handshake and certificate check will be undertaken, and the bank may undertake a further verification which will require checking the account holder database with another handshake and certificate check. If any one of these certificate checks fails, for any reason, including those outlined previously, the transaction will fail. I have had this experience myself and can see exactly where things are failing.

With respect to a single, private transaction, there will usually be some way around the problem. In the example given, the user could telephone their solicitor and arrange payment by other means. But supposing this was a major bank with potentially thousands of transactions occurring within a single hour? What if one of the primary certificates were to fail or disappear from view? By the time this has been spotted and rectified, a good deal of damage may have occurred in the form of lost payments which now have to be rescheduled, possibly one by one as the other parties involved will have assumed that the transactions had been completed. They will all need to be contacted and assured that the transactions, in fact, did not complete and now need to be resubmitted. The cost of this undertaking will be significant, not only in terms of time expended, but in brand damage and loss of confidence in the host organisation.

Consider a different scenario, this time with an airline booking system. Once again, there will be many hand-offs from the main website to subsites run by both the airline concerned and by third parties. The airline will need to reference its own customer database, its own crew and flight information, possibly a separate cargo or baggage handling system and, in many cases, it will be using a third-party reservation system, all of which will require handshakes, certificate exchanges and so on. It only needs one of these certificates to fail for the entire transaction to fail. The situation may be further complicated by communication with client devices such as tablets and mobile phones, which may, in fact, be passing erroneous information. The customer may become confused or may turn up for a flight which he hasn't actually been booked on. Once again, there will be significant time spent sorting the whole mess out, but the bigger cost will be to the reputation of the carrier concerned.

We could trawl through a long line of business and commercial examples whereby a failure in the PKI brings things to a standstill. At such times, the ability to retrieve the situation shall depend upon the expertise and experience of the dedicated PKI team, assuming that there is one. In any event, it will be an unnerving experience and, in extreme cases, could bring an organisation to a complete standstill. The cost of recovery might be more than the organisation can easily bear. Even if it does recover technically, it will incur a loss of faith and a damaged reputation which will endure for a long time. People always remember what has gone wrong before what has gone right.

This loss of reputation may be particularly damaging to high-street retailers whose branding and image is crucial to their success. If they are prevented from doing business, perhaps because the link to their payment provider has broken and they cannot resolve card or mobile phone–linked sales, this could have a very significant impact. If they happen to be a retailer who sells fresh produce, such as vegetables for example, then they have an additional risk of being over-stocked and having to dispose of their stock. If they are a mainstream retailer, situated in a key position within a town, the financial impact could also be significant. The same is true of any situation which is transaction based, from taxi services to hospital admissions which might need to cross-reference other systems.

Another very real possibility may be triggered by software developers themselves, especially if they are concerned with applications which have a security context. IT and IT Security have more recommendations and best practices than you can shake a stick at. Someone working in this area may notice something which looks like non-compliance and, consequently, make changes to parts of the code which happen to be associated with certificates, either directly or indirectly. For example, they might re-write a block of code and completely miss the fact that the previous code was making a call to an external certificate. Or perhaps, they might meddle with certificates themselves, perhaps in an attempt to align expiry dates, making some of them expire sooner than expected. The Chief Information Security Officer (CISO) role comes with a sea of recommendations around compliance, security and disaster recovery which may or may not filter down to those actually creating containers and associated code. Furthermore, as has been previously mentioned, the more container clusters and microservices one has, the less likely they are to be properly documented. One might argue that they are almost self-documenting and there is something in this; nevertheless, under a DevOps model, they could be changing quite quickly. If all of this gets into a real mess and certificates start to fail or not be recognised, or are perhaps in the wrong place, and if this broader architecture includes calls out to payment providers and banks, then the impact will be significant and, under such a scenario, finding exactly what has gone wrong may not be straightforward.

In these mostly commercial scenarios explored, the degree of impact and the cost of recovery will naturally vary according to the size and brand image of the company concerned. This degree of damage may range from mild and manageable to catastrophic. It is not an over-statement to suggest that even a large company could be put out of business by repeated PKI-related failures. It is an area that deserves close attention. If any organisation has no knowledge of whether it has certificates and, if so, where they are, then that organisation is taking a significant risk.

Now, let us extrapolate this same thinking to government agencies. Nearly all governments have outsourced their IT services to third parties. Indeed, most government IT has fallen into the hands of just two or three huge organisations. This in itself constitutes a risk. Most of these giant organisations have now moved everything into the cloud – another risk. Most of them are also crowing about microservices, containers, service meshes, sidecars and all the other Cloud Native jargon. Research for this book quickly uncovered the reality that many within these giant organisations haven't a clue about any of this. They are relying upon internal 'technology advocates' and a handful of developers who seem to be doing whatever they like. For them, it's one big playtime as they experiment with all the new goodies that others have dreamed up. Containers were supposed to seamlessly integrate PKI, but this does not seem to work. So, service meshes were supposed to be the answer, often using 'sidecars' attached to containers. But this doesn't always work either. So, special, 'cloud native' PKI management solutions have appeared in order to solve the problem once and for all. A quick trawl through the forums shows that this is not always working either. You might be lucky. Your nest of container clusters might be small enough and with few enough secure transactions for it to work. Or, you might be unlucky. You might realise that you have a problem. Or you might not realise that you have a problem. I have undertaken some simple tests with government websites and have found them to fail fairly often when trying to access one service from another. Even pages within the same department often return errors. Why? Is no one checking them? Furthermore, it varies from country to country. With some countries, I can flick through web pages with no real problem. With others, it's an endless series of cookie pop-ups followed by failed pages. On-line government applications which require multiple pages of form filling can be especially problematic. If this is the situation with public-facing material, what is the situation with important internal transactions or inter-governmental transactions? Much of this will be caused by a broken PKI.

If we consider that a badly broken PKI can bring a commercial organisation to its knees and damage its reputation irrevocably, then a similar thing can happen with respect to government IT systems. Politically, the answer will probably be to keep throwing money at the problem in the hope that it might go away. But this is rarely a satisfactory response. Then, there are the interfaces between government and commercial IT systems to consider, whether implemented via the web or directly. This may become especially problematic when one side does everything properly and the other does not.

All of this is accentuated, quite considerably, by the current penchant for the Cloud Native methodology which serves to confuse the issue. Those wise enough to maintain their own physical infrastructure will have a much better control over their PKI. Furthermore, if they have embraced the open-source model, as advocated within these pages, they will have absolute control, including over the source code, all at little or no cost to themselves. In addition, taking this route represents an excellent way to really learn about PKI, right down to fine detail. It will enable robust links with third-party certificate providers, together with absolute clarity around when to use self-signed certificates and also where every certificate is located, its expiry date and so on. Furthermore, if an external issue is discovered, it may quickly be flagged up – which, in turn, helps the other party, whoever they are. Considering the implications of certificate and PKI failure, just a glimpse of which has been provided here, the way forwards would seem an obvious one.

SUMMARY

It has been explained that PKI-related failures can, and often do, have severe consequences. In the list of possible causes provided, the author has deliberately omitted malicious causes such as the deliberate manipulation of code or certificates masquerading as legitimate when, in fact, they are fake and may fool systems into revealing information which should remain hidden. Of course, there exists an army of hackers and others who seem to do nothing but deliberately attack IT systems, whether corporate or governmental. If these people find a weak and poorly implemented PKI, they will doubtless exploit the opportunities thus provided.

Several institutions and academic groups have compiled lists of PKI-related attacks and outages. One such summary is provided below;

Incident Type	CA misinterpreted/unaware of BR	Software bug	Operational error	Human error	Business model/CA decision/testing	Non-optimal request check	Change in Baseline Requirements (BR)	Improper security controls	Inadequate audit compliance	Organizational constraints	Other[2]	No data[3]
Fields in certificates not compliant to BR	29	46	28	50	13	7	8	1	3	3	6	20
Audit report failure	25	0	9	1	13	0	1	0	3	1	2	9
Non-BR-compliant revocation information	12	12	5	2	1	0	1	0	1	0	5	1
Serial number failures	18	7	2	3	4	0	3	0	0	0	1	2
512/1024 bits key	0	1	1	0	13	0	2	0	0	0	0	8
Possible issuance of rogue certificates	1	4	0	0	3	7	0	1	0	0	0	1
Undisclosed SubCA	6	1	6	1	0	0	1	0	0	0	0	2
Delay of certificate revocation	0	0	6	1	4	0	0	0	0	1	1	1
CAA mis-issuance	2	6	0	0	1	1	0	0	0	0	0	3
Use of SHA-1/MD5 hashing algorithm	1	0	2	3	2	1	1	0	0	0	0	1
Rogue certificate	0	1	1	2	2	5	0	0	0	0	0	0
CA/RA/SubCA/Reseller hacked	0	0	0	0	1	0	0	9	0	0	0	0
Other[1]	17	9	16	10	12	4	4	0	1	2	3	3

Cause

OXFORD UNIVERSITY PRESS *J Cyber Secur*, Volume 7, Issue 1, 2021, tyab025, https://doi.org/10.1093/cybsec/tyab025

However, many, if not most, of the failures attributable to PKI failures will never be reported as organisations will not want to reveal the fact that they have suffered failures which might have been avoided. The same is true for certificate authorities who have occasionally faced serious issues. This is one of the reasons that this book is important. We must not assume that all technology is good or that changes of approach are necessarily helpful. My last words on the subject must be yet another plea to embrace the open-source model, learn how PKI really works, using open-source tools and appoint an in-house specialist team to manage it all for you. And beware of clouds. They rain down on you sometimes.

Epilogue
Summing things up

The reader is to be congratulated upon reaching this far with what has been a somewhat controversial look at public key infrastructure (PKI). It might have been expected that such a book would simply promote all of the existing technologies. That it would delve into the minutia of PKI detail. That it would provide endless examples and case studies. That it might even include exercises for the hapless reader to undertake, one after another. Yes, all of that might have been expected, but to what end? What good would that be? It would simply be a reiteration of what has been written a thousand times before. If one has an appetite for meaningless papers on the subject, one may visit almost any technology provider's web site, or even some of the government departments described in the previous chapter. There is no end to them. One may wade, waist deep in them for miles, dream about them at night, stand up and quote from them in meetings and conferences. But all to no avail. The subject will not be any better understood and people will still follow like sheep, those who promote meaningless technologies and daft ideas. So long as there are new buzz words for the faithful, so long shall they follow the herd, fearful of being seen as capable of independent thought. Of reason. Of rational deduction. Of human intelligence.

Yes, this book is different. Unashamedly so, as it seeks to uncover some of the nonsense, expose the myths and half-truths and focus upon what we should be doing and how to do it. Some may shake their heads in dismay because I have not embraced all of the latest technological ideas without giving them a thought. Some may question why I have not simply followed everyone else and reiterated all of the nice buzz words, or promoted technologies which, actually, are against the public interest. Some will be horrified because I have not embraced the centralisation, globalisation and automation model which is destroying so much of our society, our culture. Indeed, it is gnawing at the roots of civilisation itself. Harsh words? Yes. We need them. We need more of them, and we need more people to stand up and speak the truth about the use of technology in society and how to do things properly, and in the interests of normal, decent human beings.

DOI: 10.1201/9781003360674-25

Much has been written within these pages about the currently popular DevOps methodology which, to those who are being paid as technology advocates, seems like a wonderful idea. However, to those who have several decades of experience in designing, building and supporting IT in general, it does not seem so attractive. Why? Because it is trading well-considered and well-proven methodologies for something which has been created for its own sake and which is guaranteed to introduce problems and issues which we did not have previously. Furthermore, they will include issues outside of the immediate IT landscape. If there is a well-proven way of going about things, which everyone concerned understands, then why not continue with it? The simple answer is the same answer which lies behind so much of what is wrong in the world today. Greed. Pure and simple. Lobbyists corrupt government agencies and other organisations with unfounded promises of reduced costs and increased profits. Oh yes? How exactly will the adoption of DevOps lower your costs and increase your profits? The lobbyists will reply that you can cut down your staff numbers. Well, there will be an immediate cost to doing that, depending upon which country you are in. Then, there will be another cost in adopting the technology, because the lobbyists will convince you that you need to buy in their services. Then, there will be another cost because the services you bought do not fully support the operation, so you will have to buy more. Then, there will be another cost because you will have to pay for an initial period of consultancy, at very high rates, because you will not understand the new technology. Then, there will be another cost as, because you have lost your own, well-trained staff, you will have to buy in outsourced personnel to administer the new technology. Then, there will be another cost as you rebuild what you already had, but with the new technology. Then, there will be another cost when the new technology breaks and you have to call the consultants back in. And all of these costs will roll on, year on year, for as long as your organisation exists. Get the picture? Has this made your costs lower? No. Has it made your product offering any better? No. Has it made you any more profitable? No. Indeed, it is likely that many of your customers will have lost confidence in your organisation due to the technology failures which you will have undoubtedly experienced. I can see this happening all around as I write these words.

In the traditional world, the requirements for a revised or new IT application came from the business, usually after careful consideration. These requirements would be discussed with an appropriate IT project team who would be familiar with this particular business area. From these discussions a design specification would be drawn up, and this would be further discussed and approved by the business area in question. Once finalised, this design specification would be passed to the development team who would undertake the necessary coding in order to produce the finished application. This application would then be vigorously tested by the IT operations team, within a test environment which would be a carbon copy of the live environment. If anything did not work perfectly, it would be returned to the developers. Only after exhaustive testing would the application be shown to the business area in question, hopefully for their approval. Once this approval had been received, then the application would be moved into the live environment and, of course, it would work entirely as expected. If this process sounds long and drawn out, let me assure that it is not. It would not be unusual for all this to occur within the same week, or two or three weeks at the outside. But then, the application might well be used for several years. That is actually very efficient in real terms. Furthermore, as applications built this way tended not to break, it promoted confidence in both the business (from its customers) and the IT department (from the business). If any new technologies came along which seemed to be valuable, as happened with Linux for example, then these technologies would be subject to a very careful, in-depth evaluation by the IT department and, if felt potentially useful, would be tested exhaustively. Then, tested again. Then, they would be used for a while within the test environment. They would then only be used in the live environment if an obvious opportunity came along to do so. A sound approach to the introduction of any genuinely valuable technology.

This is how it should be. And this is how things operated (in good organisations) for years, and everybody was happy. So why change things? Greed. Greed and direct corruption. Individuals being 'looked after' in return for forcing through the adoption of technologies that nobody asked for, wanted or needed. And so it is with DevOps. The whole idea is daft. It is not practical to try to merge development and operation teams. What they really mean is to get rid of any proper IT operations and testing and place everything in the hands of developers. The inference is that developers have the necessary skills and intuition to be able to liaise directly with the business. They do not. They have a completely different mindset and way of thinking. Younger developers in particular will be found seriously wanting in this respect. Instead of understanding and listening to the business, they will simply try to 'sell' the business new ideas based upon the technological toys that they have been playing with. This is how so many government agencies and other organisations have been duped into using the cloud and replacing a perfectly good in-house infrastructure with one that they know nothing about. Did that lower costs? No. Did it make them any more productive? No. Of course not, because the measure of their productivity will come from the skills and direction that they have in-house, not the technology. However, their costs have all risen sharply as a result and, furthermore, these are costs which will stay with them year on year. For evermore. Why duplicate or replace your own, proven infrastructure (and the intellectual assets which it contains) with one managed by someone who you don't know, probably in a completely different part of the world? Does this make any sense at all? No it does not. Ask that passing five-year old again. Now, the organisation may make its IT staff redundant and suffer a haemorrhage of skills erosion.

The cost it saves in wages and national contributions will be dwarfed by what it loses in competency, coupled to the direct and ongoing costs of adopting this model.

This is where all of these other technologies mentioned earlier in the book become important to understand because, like the cloud, none of them offer any real operational advantage. They all introduce significant and ongoing costs. They replace traditional, hard won skills with new skills which, actually, are very shallow and promote absolutely no understanding of IT. Ask a kubernetes coder how mainframes work and see what sort of answer you get. Ask them about the recognised table forms within a proper relational database and see how they reply. Ask them about truly compiled languages. Ask them to describe the principles of object-oriented programming and inheritance. You will likely be met with a lot of blank expressions. Then, ask them about kubernetes and service meshes. What you will get is a barrage of marketing speak about theoretical advantages which are, in fact, no advantage at all and have not been proven by independent testing. Then, ask them to describe, in detail, how it all works. They will not be able to. Even some of the suppliers cannot do so – I know, I've spoken with them. Ask them an in-depth technical question, and you will be met with "we will have one of our specialists come back to you". Of course, they never will. You see, it is all theoretical and a question of technology for the sake of technology. Those who follow this path will incur huge and ongoing costs, a great deal of disruption, skills erosion in a very real sense, a weakened infrastructure with increasing failures and a loss of confidence among their users and customers. In addition, as if this was not enough, they will lose control of their IT completely (together with their data assets and intellectual property). They will no longer understand how anything works or where it is. They will not know where to look first when things break (and they *will* break). Their so-called DevOps developers, whether in-house or, more likely, outsourced, will have little or no understanding of the business in real terms. So, is it a good idea to follow this path? No it is not. Ask that five-year old again, they will explain it to you in practical, down-to-Earth terms. So why do people do this? Greed and corruption. It is destroying conventional IT and many businesses along the way. It is creating 'pretend' environments with self-congratulatory middle managers who do not know what they are doing. It is de-skilling the workforce to an alarming degree. It is destroying pride and competence. It is destroying the very fabric of our civilisation.

Those technology advocates, working at home from their tablets, will tell you that it is all marvellous because now you can put several builds a day into the live environment. But why would you want to? It is simply asking for trouble. And that is what is happening. See for yourself how many processes on the web don't work properly anymore. This is especially visible when trying to interface to banks and government agencies. Things break. All the time. They did not use to, so what is going wrong? Well, if you have got this far with the book, you will know the reason.

And so, sitting atop this technological dichotomy, we have PKI. On the one hand, it may easily be managed and kept in good order, on the other it will become chaotic, expensive and likely to break. Which would you prefer? If it is the former, then you need to regain control of your IT assets and bring them back in-house. If you still have them all in-house, then you are one step ahead. Then, you need to understand what is happening with your existing IT estate. For every single server, you need to know precisely where which certificates are stored and why. If you are using Linux (and you should be), there are defined locations where different Linux distributions place their certificate store, but these are easily found. Then, there are applications which may have their own certificates, stored in their own folders. These also need to be identified. And so on. Once every certificate is accounted for and listed in a certificate database, it will then be possible to check their attributes and ensure that they comply with whatever standard you define. Of course, their dates of expiry need to be managed, with automatic renewal where sensible and possible. And so on. The activities of a core PKI team have been well covered elsewhere in this book. All of this is straightforward and easily managed and supported on an ongoing basis, if you are using your own infrastructure, managed by your own people, who understand your organisation's operation.

If, on the other hand, you are leaving everything in the cloud and have decided to embrace the microservices, containers, service meshes and add-on approach, then, good luck. You will effectively have no control over your PKI and will no doubt end up relying on a third party who will automate everything, for better or for worse, and you will get failures and outages. In addition, you will pay through the nose for the privilege. Still, you can rest assured that you will be politically correct and able to hold your head up high at conferences where suppliers congratulate each other about *their* wonderful success. But surely, this is an exaggeration? What about all those 'case studies' that the suppliers wheel out which show how people halve their costs and double their profits? Well, who exactly is representing the 'case study' in question? The IT director? A senior developer? Whoever it is, they have surely been 'influenced' by the supplier. I have seen this so many times. And where is the evidence for their nonsensical claims? Do they show you the organisation's balance sheets and end of year accounts? And what of the intangibles such as confidence in the organisation, retained customers or the wellbeing of staff? So many organisations have been brought to their knees by improper practices with respect to IT. Outsourcing and the use of the cloud, now exacerbated by microservices, containers and service meshes, have destroyed many previously good IT departments who were doing a good job for the organisation that they represented. I have seen this at close quarters and understand all the signs.

But this is a book about PKI so why even mention these other factors? Because PKI underpins so much of it. PKI is important and, if organisations are to act in a responsible manner, then they must take the time and effort to understand PKI properly. In order to do this, they also need to understand the broader IT landscape. In gathering *this* understanding, they may discover some real horror stories. It is possible, if not probable, that they will also discover signs of outright corruption and, almost certainly, a lack of due diligence. This, in turn, affects security. Both cyber security as it has become popularly known and security with respect to the intellectual property and assets of the organisation in question. This latter factor may manifest itself in a number of ways, and the processes undertaken in order to understand the organisational PKI may uncover some of them. And so, you see, not only is PKI important in it's own right, but it may be used as a tool with which to regain a proper control over your organisation's IT and associated assets. Along the way, you will have the opportunity to define sensible policies, processes and procedures which, in turn, may be adopted by all personnel. Eventually, your organisation will emerge as a stronger, more confident entity with happier, well-trained IT personnel who are loyal to the organisation. It is not that difficult to achieve. The enemies are arrogance, ignorance, greed and corruption and, unfortunately, they are everywhere. However, once this is realised and appropriate measures are taken to combat them, then anything may be achieved.

Anything else? Yes. Embrace the open source model and use freely available open source tools, for which, unlike proprietary products, there exists a wealth of documentation and people with real-world experience who are happy to share it. If you follow this path, you will be absolutely in control and know where everything is and how everything works. Furthermore, desktop open source products have now evolved to the point where they are entirely practical and, generally, more stable than their proprietary equivalents, with all the desktop applications that you could ever wish for. Indeed, it is possible to run an entire organisation entirely on freely available open source products, if one has the will to do so. Its simple really. Ask that five-year old again. In exchange for a packet of sweets, they will probably grant you a 30-minute exchange of ideas. It will be the best 30 minutes you ever invest in.

SUMMARY

Well, the epilogue has provided a snapshot of the current, somewhat confused, IT landscape. It is a landscape in a state of flux as new ideas and technologies are sweeping in at a fast pace. Too fast for many to keep up with. But why should they feel obliged to keep up with them in the first place? This section has shown that it is not always a good idea to do so. The promises being made by technology advocates are simply not being realised in practice. The end result for many is vastly increased costs to do exactly what they were doing before they started, only now, they have also lost control of things completely. This really does not make any sense at all.

With respect to PKI, following the Emperor's new clothes approach simply complicates things by orders of magnitude. In many cases, it will increase PKI-related costs by a similar measure. And so, the primary message of this book has been to tread carefully and not to believe unsubstantiated claims by aggressive technology suppliers. Rather, to keep or regain control of your IT infrastructure and then apply PKI in a measured, intelligent manner. It is all straightforward enough, especially if you adopt open source components which are freely available and well documented. In fact, they also represent a solid training ground for your in-house IT staff. And, if you require more IT staff, hire them. There are plenty of experienced people around at the moment who would be a godsend to your organisation. I truly wish you well with your ongoing endeavours.

Julian Ashbourn
Berkhamsted, June 2022

Index

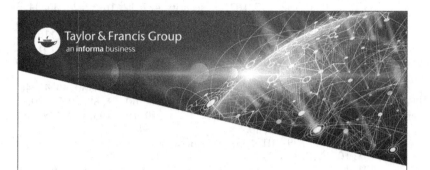

Printed in the United States
by Baker & Taylor Publisher Services

Printed in the United States
by Baker & Taylor Publisher Services